Discourse
on
Method
and
Meditations
on
First Philosophy

Discourse on Method
and
Meditations on First Philosophy

fourth edition

RENÉ DESCARTES

Translated by
DONALD A. CRESS

HACKETT PUBLISHING COMPANY
Indianapolis/Cambridge

René Descartes: 1596–1650

Discourse on Method was originally published in 1637.
Meditations on First Philosophy was originally published in 1641.

Fourth edition copyright © 1998 by Hackett Publishing Company, Inc.

17 16 15 14 13   7 8 9 10 11

All rights reserved
Printed in the United States of America

Cover design by Listenberger Design & Associates
Interior design by Dan Kirklin

For further information, please address
 Hackett Publishing Company, Inc.
 P. O. Box 44937
 Indianapolis, Indiana 46244-0937
 www.hackettpublishing.com

Library of Congress Cataloging-in-Publication Data

Descartes, René, 1596–1650.
    [Discours de la méthode. English]
    Discourse on method ; and, Meditations on first philosophy / René Descartes ; translated by Donald A. Cress.—4th ed.
        p.   cm.
    Includes bibliographical references.
    ISBN 0-87220-421-9 — ISBN 0-87220-420-0 (pbk.)
    1. Methodology. 2. Science—Methodology. 3. First philosophy.
I. Cress, Donald A. II. Descartes, René, 1596–1650. Meditations on
first philosophy. III. Title. IV. Title: Meditations on first
philosophy.
B1848.E5C73 1998b
194—dc21   98-38149
                                                                CIP

ISBN-13: 978-0-87220-421-8 (cloth)
ISBN-13: 978-0-87220-420-1 (pbk.)

CONTENTS

Editor's Preface   vii
Selected Bibliography   xi

DISCOURSE ON METHOD

Note on the Translation   xviii
PART ONE   1
PART TWO   6
PART THREE   13
PART FOUR   18
PART FIVE   23
PART SIX   33

MEDITATIONS ON FIRST PHILOSOPHY

Note on the Translation   46
Letter of Dedication   47
Preface to the Reader   51
Synopsis of the Following Six Meditations   54
MEDITATION ONE: Concerning Those Things That Can Be Called into Doubt   59
MEDITATION TWO: Concerning the Nature of the Human Mind: That It Is Better Known Than the Body   63
MEDITATION THREE: Concerning God, That He Exists   69
MEDITATION FOUR: Concerning the True and the False   81
MEDITATION FIVE: Concerning the Essence of Material Things, and Again Concerning God, That He Exists   87
MEDITATION SIX: Concerning the Existence of Material Things, and the Real Distinction between Mind and Body   92

EDITOR'S PREFACE

René Descartes was born March 31, 1596, in a small town in Touraine called La Haye (now called La Haye-Descartes or simply Descartes). When he was about ten years old, his father sent him to the Collège Henri IV at La Flèche, a newly formed school which was soon to become the showcase of Jesuit education and one of the outstanding centers for academic training in Europe. Later in his life Descartes looked with pride on the classical education he had received from the Jesuits, even though he did not always find agreeable what the Jesuits taught him. He especially found the scholastic Aristotelianism taught there distasteful, although he did cherish his training in many other disciplines—particularly mathematics.

Descartes left La Flèche in 1614 to study civil and canon law at Poitiers, and by 1616 had received the baccalaureate and licentiate degrees in law. In 1618 Descartes joined the army of Prince Maurice of Nassau as an unpaid volunteer, but apparently he never saw combat. He seems to have been more interested in using military service as a means of seeing the world.

During a tour of duty in Germany, events of lifelong importance happened to Descartes. In November of 1619 he was sitting in a *poêle*, a small stove-heated room, meditating on the disunity and uncertainty of his knowledge. He marveled at mathematics, a science in which he found certainty, necessity, and precision. How could he find a basis for all knowledge so that it might have the same unity and certainty as mathematics? Then, in a blinding flash, Descartes saw the method to be pursued for putting all the sciences, all knowledge, on a firm footing. This method made clear both how new knowledge was to be achieved and how all previous knowledge could be certain and unified. That evening Descartes had a series of dreams that seemed to put a divine stamp of approval on his project. Shortly thereafter he left military service.

Throughout the early part of his life, Descartes was plagued by a sense of impotence and frustration about the task he had set about to accomplish: a new and stable basis for all knowledge. He had the programmatic vision, but he seemed to despair of being able to work it out in detail. Thus, perhaps we have an explanation for the fact that Descartes, during much of the 1620s, threw himself into the pursuit of the good life. Travel, gambling, and dueling seemed especially to attract his attention.

This way of life ended in 1628, when, through the encouragement of Cardinal de Bérulle, Descartes decided to see his program through to completion. He left France to avoid the glamour and the social life; he renounced the distractions in which he could easily lose himself and forget what he knew to be his true calling. He departed for Holland, where he would live for the next twenty years.

It was during this period that Descartes began his *Rules for the Direction of the Mind* and wrote a short treatise on metaphysics, although the former was not published during his lifetime and the latter seems to have been destroyed by him. Much of the early 1630s was taken up with scientific questions. However, Descartes's publication plans were abruptly altered when he learned of the trial of Galileo in Rome. Descartes decided, as Aristotle had centuries before, that philosophy would not be sinned against twice. He suppressed his scientific treatise, *The World or Treatise on Light*.

In 1637 Descartes published in French a *Discourse on the Method for Conducting One's Reason Well and for Searching for Truth in the Sciences;* it introduced three treatises which were to exemplify the new method: one on optics, one on geometry, and one on meteorology. Part IV of the introductory *Discourse* contained, in somewhat sketchy form, much of the philosophical basis for constructing the new system of knowledge.

In response to queries about this section, Descartes prepared a much lengthier discussion of the philosophical underpinnings for his vision of a unified and certain body of human knowledge. This response was to be his *Meditations on First Philosophy*, completed in the spring of 1640—but not published until August, 1641. Attached to the *Meditations* were sets of objections and queries sent by readers who had read the manuscript, plus Descartes's replies to each set.

The period following the publication of the *Meditations* was marked by controversy and polemics. Aristotelians, both Catholic and Protestant, were outraged; many who did not understand Descartes's teachings took him to be an atheist and a libertine. In spite of all of this clamor, Descartes hoped that his teachings would replace those of Aristotle. To this end he published in 1644 his *Principles of Philosophy*, a four-part treatise which he hoped would supplant the Aristotelian scholastic manuals used in most universities. The last important work to be published during his lifetime was his *Passions of the Soul*, in which Descartes explored such topics as the relationship of the soul to the body, the nature of emotion, and the role of the will in controlling the emotions.

In 1649 Queen Christina of Sweden convinced Descartes that he should come to Stockholm in order to teach her philosophy. Christina seems to have regarded Descartes more as a court ornament for her amusement and edification than as a serious philosopher; however, it was the brutal winter of 1649 that proved to be Descartes's undoing. Of the climate in Sweden Descartes was to say: "It seems to me that men's thoughts freeze here during winter, just as does the water." Descartes was stricken with pneumonia early in February of 1650 and, after more than a week of suffering, died on February 11.

SELECTED BIBLIOGRAPHY

A. STANDARD EDITION

Oeuvres de Descartes, publiés par Charles Adam et Paul Tannery, 13 volumes. Paris: Cerf, 1897–1913. (Vols. 1–11 contain Descartes's writings; vol. 12 contains Charles Adam's *Vie et oeuvres de Descartes*; vol. 13 is a supplementary volume containing correspondence, biographical material, and various indexes.) It has been updated (Paris: Vrin, 1996), and additional correspondence has been appended to various volumes. More accurate identifications of dates and addressees have been supplied; especially important is the inclusion of Descartes's correspondence with Huygens. This edition is commonly cited as AT.

B. ENGLISH TRANSLATIONS

The Philosophical Works of Descartes. 2 volumes. Rendered into English by Elizabeth S. Haldane and G.R.T. Ross. 2nd edition, corrected. Cambridge: Cambridge University Press, 1931.

> Until 1984 this often reprinted but error-plagued set of volumes was the standard translation of many of Descartes's central works. Virtually all twentieth-century Anglo-American scholars made use of Haldane-Ross. This edition was commonly cited as HR.

The Philosophical Writings of Descartes. 3 vols. Translated by John Cottingham, Robert Stoothoff, Dugald Murdoch, and Anthony Kenny. Cambridge: Cambridge University Press, 1984, 1991.

> This translation is a welcome replacement of HR. The first volume contains philosophical works other than those related to the *Meditations*; the second volume contains the *Meditations* and the *Replies to Objections*; the third volume contains Descartes's philosophical correspondence and much of the *Conversation with Burman*. This edition is commonly cited as CSM.

Descartes, Philosophical Letters, Edited and translated by Anthony Kenny. Oxford: Oxford University Press, 1970; reprinted Minneapolis: University of Minnesota, 1981.

> Descartes's correspondence is an invaluable resource that complements his published works. For twenty years this was the standard English translation of Descartes's philosophical correspondence. Although the translations are reliable, references in the footnotes and the index should be used with care, as there are many errors in the Oxford edition, and they were not corrected in the later reprint. This volume was commonly cited as K. It has now been incorporated into volume three of CSM; errors have been corrected, and additional correspondence has been included.

Descartes' Conversation with Burman. Translated, with notes, by John Cottingham. Oxford: Oxford University Press, 1976.

> Housed in the Library of the University of Göttingen is a manuscript that purports to chronicle a discussion between Descartes and the young Dutch theologian Francis Burman. Burman had chosen several texts from Descartes' writings for discussion. Sometimes he would criticize the doctrine in the text; sometimes he would simply ask for clarification. Descartes' (?) replies are always interesting and nearly always shed light on difficult passages in his published works. Cottingham's extensive commentary is both interesting and helpful. It is commonly cited as CB. Since volume three of CSM does not provide the complete text of the *Conversation with Burman*, this translation must continue to be consulted.

Discourse on Method, Optics, Geometry, and Meteorology. Translated by Paul J. Olscamp. Indianapolis: Bobbs-Merrill, 1965.

Treatise on Man. French text with translation and commentary by Thomas Steele Hall. Cambridge: Harvard University Press, 1972.

Descartes: Le Monde, ou Traité de la lumière. Translation and introduction by Michael Sean Mahoney. New York: Abaris Books. 1979.

Descartes: Principles of Philosophy. Translated, with explanatory notes, by Valentine Rodger Miller and Reese P. Miller. Dordrecht: Reidel, 1983.

The Passions of the Soul. Translated by Stephen Voss. Indianapolis: Hackett Publishing Company, 1989.

C. BIBLIOGRAPHIES: 1800–1984

Sebba, Gregor. *Bibliographia Cartesiana: A Critical Guide to the Descartes Literature 1800–1960*. The Hague: Nijoff, 1964.

> This is the basic bibliographical tool of pre-1960 Descartes scholarship. It contains a large number of annotations and cross-references; it is well indexed by person and subject matter. Although somewhat weak in its coverage of twentieth-century Anglo-American analytical literature on Descartes, it is outstanding in its coverage of continental scholarship.

Doney, Willis. "Bibliography," in *Descartes: A Collectum of Critical Essays*. New York: Doubleday, 1967, pp. 369–386.

> This bibliography largely rectifies Sebba's lack of coverage of pre-1960 analytical works on Descartes. It is concerned chiefly with English titles; it is divided by subject matter.

Chappell, Vere, and Willis Doney. *Twenty-Five Years of Descartes Scholarship, 1960–1984: A Bibliography*. New York: Garland, 1987.

> This volume, while neither complete nor adequately indexed, is still the best update of Sebba.

Armogathe, Robert, Vincent Carraud and Massimiliano Savini. *Bibliographie cartésienne (1960–1996)*. Lecce: Conte, 2003.

Cress, Donald A. "Canadian and American Dissertations on Descartes and Cartesianism: 1865–1984." *Philosophy Research Archives* 13 (April 1988).

> This bibliography provides author, title, university, and location in *Dissertation Abstracts International*, as well as the University Microfilms International order number, when available.

Gabel, Gernot U. *Descartes: A List of Doctoral Dissertations Accepted by Universities in Western Europe and North America 1885–2000*. Hürth: Edition Gemini, 2006.

D. BOOKS ON DESCARTES

Alanen, Lilli. *Descartes's Concept of Mind*. Cambridge, Mass.: Harvard University Press, 2003.

Almog, Joseph. *What Am I?: Descartes and the Mind-Body Problem*. New York: Oxford University Press, 2002.

Ariew, Roger. *Descartes's Metaphysical Reasoning*. New York: Routledge, 2001.

Ariew, Roger, John Cottingham, and Tom Sorell (eds.). *Descartes' Meditations: Background Source Materials*. New York: Cambridge University Press, 1998.

Baker, Gordon, and Katherine J. Morris. *Descartes' Dualism*. New York: Routledge, 1996.

Beck, Leslie. *The Metaphysics of Descartes*. Oxford: Oxford University Press, 1965.

Bracken, Harry M. *Descartes*. Oxford: Oneworld, 2002.

Broughton, Janet. *Descartes's Method of Doubt*. Princeton: Princeton University Press, 2002.

Broughton, Janet, and John Peter Carriero. *A Companion to Descartes*. Malden, MA: Blackwell, 2008.

Butler, R. J., ed. *Cartesian Essays*. Oxford: Basil Blackwell, 1972.

Carriero, John Peter. *Between Two Worlds: A Reading of Descartes's Meditations*. Princeton: Princeton University Press, 2009.

Caton, Hiram. *The Origin of Subjectivity: An Essay on Descartes*. New Haven: Yale University Press, 1973.

Chappell, Vere, ed. *Essays on Early Modern Philosophy from Descartes and Hobbes to Newton and Leibniz*. Vol. I: René Descartes. New York: Garland, 1992.

Chappell, Vere. *Descartes's Meditations: Critical Essays*. Lanham, MD: Rowman & Littlefield, 1997.

Clarke, Desmond. *Descartes: A Biography*. New York: Cambridge University Press, 2006.

Cottingham, John. *Descartes*. Oxford: Basil Blackwell, 1986.

Cottingham, John, ed. *The Cambridge Companion to Descartes*. New York: Cambridge University Press, 1992.

Cottingham, John, ed. *A Descartes Dictionary*. Oxford: Oxford University Press, 1994.

Cottingham, John, ed. *Reason, Will, and Sensation: Studies in Descartes' Metaphysics*. Oxford: Clarendon Press, 1994.

Cottingham, John. *Descartes*. New York: Oxford University Press, 1998.

Cottingham, John. *Cartesian Reflection*. New York: Oxford University Press, 2008.

Curley, E. M. *Descartes against the Sceptics*. Cambridge, Mass.: Harvard University Press, 1978.

Dicker, Georges. *Descartes, An Analytical and Historical Introduction*. Oxford: Oxford University Press, 1993.

Doney, Willis, ed. *Descartes, A Collection of Critical Essays*. Garden City: Doubleday, 1967.

Doney, Willis, ed. *Eternal Truths and the Cartesian 'Circle': A Collection of Studies*. New York: Garland, 1987.

Flage, Daniel, & Clarence Bonnen. *Descartes and Method: A Search for a Method in the Meditations*. New York: Routledge, 1999.

Francks, Richard. *Descartes' Meditations: A Reader's Guide*. New York: Continuum, 2008.

Frankfurt, Harry G. *Demons, Dreamers, and Madmen: The Defense of Reason in Descartes's Meditations*. Indianapolis: Bobbs-Merrill, 1970; reprinted New York: Garland, 1987.

Garber, Daniel. *Descartes' Metaphysical Physics*. Chicago: University of Chicago Press, 1992.

Gaukroger, Stephen. *Descartes: An Intellectual Biography*. New York: Oxford University Press, 1995.

Gibson, A. Boyce. *The Philosophy of Descartes*. London: Methuen and Co., 1932; reprinted New York: Garland, 1987.

Gilson, Étienne. *Discours de la méthode: texte et commentaire*. 4th edition. Paris: Vrin, 1967.

Grayling, A. C. *Descartes: The Life and Times of a Genius*. New York: Walker and Company, 2006.

Grene, Marjorie. *Descartes*. Minneapolis: University of Minnesota Press, 1985; reprint, Indianapolis/Cambridge: Hackett Publishing Company, 1997.

Gombay, André. *Descartes*. Malden, MA: Blackwell, 2007.

Gueroult, Martial. *Descartes' Philosophy Interpreted According to the Order of Reasons*. 2 vols. Translated by Roger Ariew. Minneapolis: University of Minnesota Press, 1984, 1985.

Selected Bibliography

Hatfield, Gary. *Routledge Philosophy Guidebook to Descartes and The Meditations.* New York: Routledge, 2003.

Hoffman, Paul. *Essays on Descartes.* New York: Oxford University Press, 2009.

Hooker, Michael, ed. *Descartes, Critical and Interpretive Essays.* Baltimore: Johns Hopkins University Press, 1978.

Janowski, Zbigniew. *Cartesian Theodicy: Descartes' Quest for Certitude.* Boston: Kluwer Academic, 2000.

Judovitz, Dalia. *Subjectivity and Representation in Descartes: The Origins of Modernity.* New York: Cambridge University Press, 1988.

Kenny, Anthony. *Descartes: A Study of His Philosophy.* New York: Random House, 1968; reprinted New York: Garland, 1987.

Marion, Jean-Luc. *Cartesian Questions: Method and Metaphysics.* Chicago: University of Chicago Press, 1999.

Markie, Peter J. *Descartes's Gambit.* Ithaca: Cornell University Press, 1986.

Matthews, Gareth B. *Thought's Ego in Augustine and Descartes.* Ithaca: Cornell University Press, 1992.

Menn, Stephen. *Descartes and Augustine.* New York: Cambridge University Press, 1998.

Moyal, Georges J. D., ed. *René Descartes: Critical Assessments.* 4 vols. New York: Routledge, 1991.

Osler, Margaret J. *Divine Will and the Mechanical Philosophy.* New York: Cambridge, 1994.

Prado, C. G. *Starting with Descartes.* New York: Continuum, 2009.

Rodis-Lewis, Geneviève. *Descartes: His Life and Thought.* Ithaca: Cornell University Press, 1999.

Rorty, Amélie Oksenberg, ed. *Essays on Descartes' Meditations.* Berkeley: University of California Press, 1986.

Rubin, Ronald. *Silencing the Demon's Advocate: The Strategy of Descartes' Meditations.* Stanford: Stanford University Press, 2008.

Sepper, Dennis L. *Descartes's Imagination: Proportion, Images, and the Activity of Thinking.* Berkeley: University of California Press, 1996.

Sesonske, Alexander, and Noel Fleming, eds. *Meta-Meditations: Studies in Descartes.* Belmont: Wadsworth Publishing Co., 1965.

Sorell, Tom. *Descartes.* Oxford: Oxford University Press, 1987.

Southwell, Gareth. *A Beginner's Guide to Descartes's Meditations.* Malden, MA: Blackwell, 2008.

Tweyman, Stanley, ed. *René Descartes: Meditations on First Philosophy in Focus.* New York: Routledge, 1993.

Verbeek, Theo. *Early Reactions to Cartesian Philosophy: 1637–1650.* Carbondale: Southern Illinois University Press, 1992.

Voss, Stephen, ed. *Essays on the Philosophy and Science of René Descartes.* Oxford: Oxford University Press, 1992.

Watson, Richard A. *The Breakdown of Cartesian Metaphysics.* Atlantic Highlands, N.J.: Humanities Press International; 1987 reprint. Indianapolis/Cambridge: Hackett Publishing Company, 1998.

———. *Cogito Ergo Sum: The Life of René Descartes.* Boston: Godine, 2002.

Williams, Bernard. *Descartes, the Project of Pure Enquiry.* London: Penguin Books, 1978.

Wilson, Catherine. *Descartes's Meditations: An Introduction.* New York: Cambridge University Press, 2003.

Wilson, Margaret. *Descartes.* London: Routledge and Kegan Paul, 1978.

Wolf-Devine, Celia. *Descartes on Seeing: Epistemology and Visual Perception.* Carbondale: Southern Illinois University Press, 1993.

Discourse on the Method for Conducting One's Reason Well and for Seeking Truth in the Sciences

NOTE ON THE TRANSLATION

The translation is based on the original French version (1637) of the *Discourse on Method* found in volume six of the Adam and Tannery edition of Descartes' works (Paris: Vrin, 1965). The numbers in the margins of this translation refer to the pagination of the Adam and Tannery edition.

D.A.C.

DISCOURSE ON THE METHOD FOR CONDUCTING ONE'S REASON WELL AND FOR SEEKING THE TRUTH IN THE SCIENCES

If this discourse seems too long to be read at one time, it may be divided into six parts. In the first part, you will find various considerations concerning the sciences; in the second part, the chief rules of the method which the author has sought; in the third part, some of the rules of morality which he has derived from this method; in the fourth part, the arguments by which he proves the existence of God and of the human soul, which are the foundations of his metaphysics; in the fifth part, the order of the questions in physics that he has investigated, and particularly the explanation of the movement of the heart and of other difficulties that pertain to medicine, as well as the difference between our soul and that of beasts; and in the final part, what things the author believes are required in order to advance further in the investigation of nature than the author has done, and what reasons have made him write.

Part One

Good sense is the best distributed thing in the world, for everyone thinks himself to be so well endowed with it that even those who are the most difficult to please in everything else are not at all wont to desire more of it than they have. It is not likely that everyone is mistaken in this. Rather, it provides evidence that the power of judging well and of distinguishing the true from the false (which is, properly speaking, what people call "good sense" or "reason") is naturally equal in all men, and that the diversity of our opinions does not arise from the fact that some people are more reasonable than others, but solely from the fact that we lead our thoughts along different paths and do not take the same things into consideration. For it is not enough to have a good mind; the main thing is to apply it well. The greatest souls are capable of the greatest vices as well as of the greatest virtues. And those who proceed only very slowly can make much greater progress, provided they always follow the right path, than do those who hurry and stray from it.

For myself, I have never presumed that my mind was in any respect more perfect than that of ordinary men. In fact, I have often desired to have as quick a wit, or as keen and distinct an imagination, or as full and responsive a memory as some other people. And other than these I know of no qualities that serve in the perfecting of the mind, for as to reason or sense, inasmuch as it alone makes us men and distinguishes us from the beasts, I prefer to believe that it exists whole and entire in each of us, and in this to follow the opinion commonly held by the philosophers, who say that there are differences of degree only between accidents, but not at all between forms or natures of individuals of the same species.

But I shall have no fear of saying that I think I have been rather fortunate to have, since my youth, found myself on certain paths that have led me to considerations and maxims from which I have formed a method by which, it seems to me, I have the means to increase my knowledge by degrees and to raise it little by little to the highest point which the mediocrity of my mind and the short duration of my life will be able to allow it to attain. For I have already reaped from it such a harvest that, although I try, in judgments I make of myself, always to lean more on the side of diffidence than of presumption, and although, looking with a philosopher's eye at the various actions and enterprises of all men, there is hardly one of them that does not seem to me vain and useless, I cannot but take immense satisfaction in the progress that I think I have already made in the search for truth, and I cannot but envisage such hopes for the future that if, among the occupations of men purely as men, there is one that is solidly good and important, I dare to believe that it is the one I have chosen.

All the same, it could be that I am mistaken, and what I take for gold and diamonds is perhaps nothing but a bit of copper and glass. I know how much we are prone to err in what affects us, and also how much the judgments made by our friends should be distrusted when these judgments are in our favor. But I will be very happy to show in this discourse what paths I have followed and to represent my life in it as if in a picture, so that everyone may judge it for himself; and thus, that, learning from the common response the opinions one will have of it, this may be a new means of teaching myself, which I shall add to those that I am accustomed to using.

Thus my purpose here is not to teach the method that everyone ought to follow in order to conduct his reason well, but merely to show how I have tried to conduct my own. Those who take it upon themselves to give precepts must regard themselves as more competent than those to whom they give them; and if they are found wanting in the least detail, they are to blame. But putting forward this essay merely as a story or, if you prefer, as a fable in which, among some examples one can imitate, one will perhaps also find many others which one will have reason not to follow, I hope that it will be useful to some without being harmful to anyone, and that everyone will be grateful to me for my frankness.

I have been nourished on letters since my childhood, and because I was convinced that by means of them one could acquire a clear and assured knowledge of everything that is useful in life, I had a tremendous desire to master them. But as soon as I had completed this entire course of study, at the end of which one is ordinarily received into the ranks of the learned, I completely changed my mind. For I found myself confounded by so many doubts and errors that it seemed to me that I had not gained any profit from my attempt to teach myself, except that more and more I had discovered my ignorance. And yet I was at one of the most renowned schools of Europe, where I thought there must be learned men, if in fact any such men existed anywhere on earth. There I had learned everything the others were learning; and, not content with the disciplines we were taught there, I had gone through all the books I could lay my hands on that treated those disciplines considered the most curious and most unusual. Moreover, I knew what judgments the others were making about me; and I did not at all see that I was rated inferior to my fellow students, even though there already were some among them who were destined to take the place of our teachers. And finally our age seemed to me to be just as flourishing and as fertile in good minds as any of the preceding ones. This made me feel free to judge all others by myself, and to think that there was no doctrine in the world that was of the sort that I had previously been led to hope for.

I did not, however, cease to hold in high regard the academic exercises with which we occupy ourselves in the schools. I knew that the languages learned there are necessary for the understanding of classical texts; that the charm of fables awakens the mind; that the memorable deeds recounted in histories uplift it, and, if read with discretion, aid in forming one's judgment; that the reading of all good books is like a conversation with the most honorable people of past ages, who were their authors, indeed, even like a set conversation in which they reveal to us only the best of their thoughts; that oratory has incomparable power and beauty; that poetry has quite ravishing delicacy and sweetness; that mathematics has some very subtle stratagems that can serve as much to satisfy the curious as to facilitate all the arts and to lessen men's labor; that writings dealing with morals contain many lessons and many exhortations to virtue that are very useful; that theology teaches one how to reach heaven; that philosophy provides the means of speaking plausibly about all things and of making oneself admired by the less learned; that jurisprudence, medicine, and the other sciences bring honors and riches to those who cultivate them; and, finally, that it is good to have examined all these disciplines, even the most superstition-ridden and the most false of them, in order to know their true worth and to guard against being deceived by them.

But I believed I had already given enough time to languages, and also to the reading of classical texts, both to their histories and to their fables. For conversing with those of other ages is about the same thing as traveling. It is good to know something of the customs of various peoples, so as to judge our own more soundly and so as not to think that everything that is contrary to our ways is ridiculous and against reason, as those who have seen nothing have a habit of doing. But when one takes too much time traveling, one eventually becomes a stranger in one's own country; and when one is too curious about what commonly took place in past ages, one usually remains quite ignorant of what is taking place in one's own country. Moreover, fables make one imagine many events to be possible which are not so at all. And even the most accurate histories, if they neither alter nor exaggerate the significance of things in order to render them more worthy of being read, almost always at least omit the baser and less noteworthy details. Consequently the rest do not appear as they really are, and those who govern their own conduct by means of examples drawn from these texts are liable to fall into the extravagances of the knights of our romances and to conceive plans that are beyond their powers.

I held oratory in high regard and was enamored of poetry, but I thought both were gifts of the mind, rather than fruits of study. Those who possess the strongest reasoning and who best order their thoughts in order to make them clear and intelligible can always best persuade others of what they are proposing, even if they were to speak only Low Breton[1] and had never learned rhetoric. And those who have the most pleasing rhetorical devices and who know how to express themselves with the most embellishment and sweetness would not fail to be the greatest poets, even if the art of poetry were unknown to them.

I delighted most of all in mathematics because of the certainty and the evidence of its reasonings. But I did not yet notice its true use, and, thinking that it was of service merely to the mechanical arts, I was astonished by the fact that no one had built anything more noble upon its foundations,

---

1. This dialect was considered rather barbarous and hardly suitable for sophisticated literary endeavors.

given that they were so solid and firm. On the other hand, I compared the writings of the ancient pagans that deal with morals to very proud and very magnificent palaces that were built on nothing but sand and mud. They place virtues on a high plateau and make them appear to be valued more than anything else in the world, but they do not sufficiently instruct us about how to recognize them; and often what they call by so fine-sounding a name is nothing more than a kind of insensibility, pride, desperation, or parricide.

I revered our theology, and I desired as much as anyone else to reach heaven; but having learned as something very certain that the road to heaven is open no less to the most ignorant than to the most learned, and that the revealed truths guiding us there are beyond our understanding, I would not have dared to submit them to the frailty of my reasonings. And I thought that, in order to undertake an examination of these truths and to succeed in doing so, it would be necessary to have some extraordinary assistance from heaven and to be more than a man.

Concerning philosophy I shall say only that, seeing that it has been cultivated for many centuries by the most excellent minds that have ever lived and that, nevertheless, there still is nothing in it about which there is not some dispute, and consequently nothing that is not doubtful, I was not at all so presumptuous as to hope to fare any better there than the others; and that, considering how many opinions there can be about the very same matter that are held by learned people without there ever being the possibility of more than one opinion being true, I deemed everything that was merely probable to be well-nigh false.

Then, as for the other sciences, I judged that, insofar as they borrow their principles from philosophy, one could not have built anything solid upon such unstable foundations. And neither the honor nor the monetary gain they promised was sufficient to induce me to master them, for I did not perceive myself, thank God, to be in a condition that obliged me to make a career out of science in order to enhance my fortune. And although I did not make a point of rejecting glory after the manner of a Cynic, nevertheless I placed very little value on the glory that I could not hope to acquire except through false pretenses. And finally, as to the false doctrines, I thought I already knew well enough what they were worth, so as not to be liable to be deceived either by the promises of an alchemist, the predictions of an astrologer, the tricks of a magician, or the ruses or boasts of any of those who profess to know more than they do.

That is why, as soon as age permitted me to emerge from the supervision of my teachers, I completely abandoned the study of letters. And resolving to search for no knowledge other than what could be found within myself, or else in the great book of the world, I spent the rest of my youth traveling, seeing courts and armies, mingling with people of diverse temperaments and circumstances, gathering various experiences, testing myself in the encounters that fortune offered me, and everywhere engaging in such reflection upon the things that presented themselves that I was able to derive some profit from them. For it seemed to me that I could find much more truth in the reasonings that each person makes concerning matters that are important to him, and whose outcome ought to cost him dearly later on if he has judged badly, than in those reasonings engaged in by a man of letters in his study, which touch on speculations that produce no effect and are of no consequence to him except perhaps that, the more they are removed from common sense, the more pride he will take in them, for he will have to employ that much more wit and ingenuity in attempting to render them plausible. And I have always had an especially great desire to learn to distinguish the true from the false, in order to see my way clearly in my actions, and to go forward with confidence in this life.

It is true that, so long as I merely considered the customs of other men, I found hardly anything there about which to be confident, and that I noticed there was about as much diversity as I had previously found among the opinions of philosophers. Thus the greatest profit I derived from this was that, on seeing many things that, although they seem to us very extravagant and ridiculous, do not cease to be commonly accepted and approved among other great peoples, I learned not to believe anything too firmly of which I had been persuaded only by example and custom; and thus I little by little freed myself from many errors that can darken our natural light and render us less able to listen to reason. But after I had spent some years thus studying in the book of the world and in trying to gain some experience, I resolved one day to study within myself too and to spend all the powers of my mind in choosing the paths that I should follow. In this I had much more success, it seems to me, than had I never left either my country or my books.

Part Two

I was then in Germany, where the occasion of the wars which are not yet over there[2] had called me; and as I was returning to the army from the coronation of the emperor, the onset of winter detained me in quarters where, finding no conversation to divert me and fortunately having no worries or passions to trouble me, I remained for an entire day shut up

---

2. The Thirty Years' War (1618–48).

by myself in a stove-heated room,[3] where I was completely free to converse with myself about my thoughts. Among them, one of the first was that it occurred to me to consider that there is often not so much perfection in works composed of many pieces and made by the hands of various master craftsmen as there is in those works on which but a single individual has worked. Thus one sees that buildings undertaken and completed by a single architect are usually more attractive and better ordered than those which many architects have tried to patch up by using old walls that had been built for other purposes. Thus those ancient cities that were once mere villages and in the course of time have become large towns are usually so poorly laid out, compared to those well-ordered places that an engineer traces out on a vacant plain as it suits his fancy, that even though, upon considering each building one by one in the former sort, one often finds as much, if not more, art than one finds in those of the latter sort, still, upon seeing how the buildings are arranged—here a large one, there a small one—and how they make the streets crooked and uneven, one would say that it is chance rather than the will of some men using reason that has arranged them thus. And if one considers that there have nevertheless always been officials responsible for seeing that private buildings contribute to the attractiveness of public areas, one will well understand that it is difficult to make things that are very finely crafted by laboring only on the works of others. Thus I imagined that peoples who, having once been half savages and having been civilized only little by little, have made their laws only to the extent that the inconvenience due to crimes and quarrels have forced them to do so, could not be as well ordered as those who, from the very beginning of their coming together, have followed the fundamental precepts of some prudent legislator. Likewise, it is quite certain that the state of the true religion, whose ordinances were made by God alone, must be incomparably better ordered than all the others. And, speaking of things human, I believe that if Sparta was at one time very flourishing, this was not because of the goodness of each one of its laws taken by itself, seeing that many of them were very strange and even contrary to good morals, but because, having been devised by a single individual, they all tended toward the same end. And thus I thought that book learning, at least the kind whose reasonings are merely probable and that do not have any demonstrations, having been composed and enlarged little by little from the opinions of many different persons, does not draw nearly so close to the truth as the simple reasonings

12

---

3. There is no need to allege that Descartes sat in or on a stove. A *poêle* is simply a room heated by an earthenware stove. Cf. E. Gilson, *Discours de la méthode: texte et commentaire*, 4th edition (Paris: Vrin, 1967), p. 157.

13 that a man of good sense can naturally make about the things he encounters. And thus, too, I thought that, because we were all children before being men and because for a long time it was necessary for us to be governed by our appetites and our teachers (which were frequently in conflict with one another, and of which perhaps neither always gave us the best advice), it is nearly impossible for our judgments to be as pure or as solid as they would have been if we had had the full use of our reason from the moment of our birth and if we had always been guided by it alone.

It is true that we never see anyone pulling down all the houses in a city for the sole purpose of rebuilding them in a different style and of making the streets more attractive; but one does see very well that many people tear down their own houses in order to rebuild them, and that in some cases they are even forced to do so when their houses are in danger of collapsing and when the foundations are not very secure. This example persuaded me that it would not really be at all reasonable for a single individual to plan to reform a state by changing everything in it from the foundations up and by toppling it in order to set it up again, nor even also to reform the body of the sciences or the order established in the schools for teaching them; but that, as regards all the opinions to which I had until now given credence, I could not do better than to try to get rid of them once and for all, in order to replace them later on, either with 14 other ones that are better, or even with the same ones once I had reconciled them to the norms of reason. And I firmly believed that by this means I would succeed in conducting my life much better than if I were to build only upon old foundations and if I were to rely only on the principles of which I had allowed myself to be persuaded in my youth without ever having examined whether they were true. For although I noticed various difficulties in this undertaking, still they were not irremediable, nor were they comparable to those difficulties occurring in the reform of the least things that affect the public. These great bodies are too difficult to raise up once they have been knocked down, or even to hold up once they have been shaken; and their fall can only be very violent. Moreover, as to their imperfections, if they have any (and the mere fact of the diversity that exists among them suffices to assure one that many do have imperfections), custom has doubtless greatly mitigated them and has even prevented or imperceptibly corrected many of them, against which prudence could not provide so well. And finally, these imperfections are almost always more tolerable than changing them would be; similarly, the great roads that wind through mountains little by little become so smooth and so convenient by dint of being frequently used, that it is much better to follow them than to try to take a more direct route by climbing over rocks and descending to the bottom of precipices.

That is why I could in no way approve of those troublemaking and restless personalities who, called neither by their birth nor by their fortune to manage public affairs, are forever coming up with an idea for some new reform in this matter. And if I thought there were in this writing the slightest thing by means of which one might suspect me of such folly, I would be very sorry to permit its publication. My plan has never gone beyond trying to reform my own thoughts and building upon a foundation which is completely my own. And if, my work having pleased me sufficiently, I here show you a model of it, it is not for the reason that I would wish to advise anyone to imitate it. Perhaps those with whom God has better shared his graces will have more lofty plans; but I fear that even this one here may already be too daring for many. The single resolution to rid oneself of all the opinions to which one has heretofore given credence is not an example that everyone ought to follow; and the world consists almost exclusively of two kinds of minds for whom it is not at all suitable. First, there are those who, believing themselves more capable than they are, are unable to avoid being hasty in their judgments or to have enough patience to conduct all their thoughts in an orderly manner; as a result, if they have once taken the liberty of doubting the principles they had accepted and of straying from the common path, they could never keep to the path one must take in order to go in a more straightforward direction, and they would remain lost all their lives. Second, there are those who have enough reason or modesty to judge that they are less capable of distinguishing the true from the false than certain others by whom they can be instructed; they should content themselves more with following the opinions of these others than with looking for better ones themselves.

And as for myself, I would unquestionably have been counted among these latter persons if I had always had only one master or if I had not known at all the differences that have always existed among the opinions of the most learned. But I had learned in my college days that one cannot imagine anything so strange or so little believable that it had not been said by one of the philosophers, and since then, I had recognized in my travels that all those who have sentiments quite contrary to our own are not for that reason barbarians or savages, but that many of them use their reason as much as or more than we do. And I considered how one and the same man with the very same mind, were he brought up from infancy among the French or the Germans, would become different from what he would be had he always lived among the Chinese or the cannibals, and how, even down to the styles of our clothing, the same thing that pleased us ten years ago, and that perhaps will again please us ten years hence, now seems to us extravagant and ridiculous. Thus it is more custom and example that persuades us than any certain knowledge; and yet the majority opinion is worthless as a proof of truths that are at all difficult to discover, since it is much more likely that one man would have found them than a whole multitude of people. Hence I could not choose anyone whose opinions seemed to me should be preferred over those of the others, and I found myself, as it were, constrained to try to guide myself on my own.

But, like a man who walks alone and in the dark, I resolved to go so slowly and to use so much circumspection in all things that, if I advanced only very slightly, at least I would effectively keep myself from falling. Nor did I want to begin to reject totally any of the opinions that had once been able to slip into my head without having been introduced there by reason, until I had first spent sufficient time planning the work I was undertaking and seeking the true method for arriving at the knowledge of everything of which my mind would be capable.

When I was younger, I had studied, among the parts of philosophy, a little logic, and among those of mathematics, a bit of geometrical analysis and algebra—three arts or sciences that, it seemed, ought to contribute something to my plan. But in examining them, I noticed that, in the case of logic, its syllogisms and the greater part of its other lessons served more to explain to someone else the things one knows, or even, like the art of Lully,[4] to speak without judgment concerning matters about which one is ignorant, than to learn them. And although, in effect, it might well contain many very true and very good precepts, nevertheless there are so many others mixed up with them that are either harmful or superfluous, that it is almost as difficult to separate the latter precepts from the former as it is to draw a Diana or a Minerva from a block of marble that has not yet been hewn. Then, as to the analysis of the ancients and the algebra of the moderns, apart from the fact that they apply only to very abstract matters and seem to be of no use, the former is always so closely tied to the consideration of figures that it cannot exercise the understanding without greatly fatiguing the imagination; and in the case of the latter, one is so subjected to certain rules and to certain symbols, that out of it there results a confused and obscure art that encumbers the mind, rather than a science that cultivates it. That is why I thought it necessary to search for some other method embracing the advantages of these three yet free from their defects. And since the multiplicity of laws often provides

---

4. Ramon Llull (ca. 1236–1315), Catalan philosopher and Franciscan who wrote in defense of Christianity against the Moors by attempting to demonstrate the articles of faith by means of logic. Descartes seems to have encountered a Lullist in Dordrecht who could hold forth on any subject whatever for long periods of time. This encounter, more than any direct contact with the writings of Lull, seems to have colored Descartes' understanding of the "art of Lully." Cf. E. Gilson, *Discours de la méthode: texte et commentaire*, pp. 185–86.

excuses for vices, so that a state is much better ruled when it has but very few laws and when these are very strictly observed; likewise, in place of the large number of precepts of which logic is composed, I believed that the following four rules would be sufficient for me, provided I made a firm and constant resolution not even once to fail to observe them:

The first was never to accept anything as true that I did not plainly know to be such; that is to say, carefully to avoid hasty judgment and prejudice; and to include nothing more in my judgments than what presented itself to my mind so clearly and so distinctly that I had no occasion to call it in doubt.

The second, to divide each of the difficulties I would examine into as many parts as possible and as was required in order better to resolve them.

The third, to conduct my thoughts in an orderly fashion, by commencing with those objects that are simplest and easiest to know, in order to ascend little by little, as by degrees, to the knowledge of the most composite things, and by supposing an order even among those things that do not naturally precede one another.

And the last, everywhere to make enumerations so complete and reviews so general that I was assured of having omitted nothing.

Those long chains of utterly simple and easy reasonings that geometers commonly use to arrive at their most difficult demonstrations had given me occasion to imagine that all the things that can fall within human knowledge follow from one another in the same way, and that, provided only that one abstain from accepting any of them as true that is not true, and that one always adheres to the order one must follow in deducing the ones from the others, there cannot be any that are so remote that they are not eventually reached nor so hidden that they are not discovered. And I was not very worried about trying to find out which of them it would be necessary to begin with; for I already knew that it was with the simplest and easiest to know. And considering that, of all those who have hitherto searched for the truth in the sciences, only mathematicians have been able to find any demonstrations, that is to say, certain and evident reasonings, I did not at all doubt that it was with these same things that they had examined [that I should begin]; although I expected from them no other utility but that they would accustom my mind to nourish itself on truths and not to be content with false reasonings. But it was not my plan on that account to try to learn all those particular sciences commonly called "mathematical"; and seeing that, even though their objects differed, these sciences did not cease to be all in accord with one another in considering nothing but the various relations or proportions which are found in their objects, I thought it would be more worthwhile for me to examine only these proportions in general, and to suppose them to be only in subjects that would help me make the knowledge of them easier, and without at the same time in any way restricting them to those subjects, so that later I could apply them all the better to everything else to which they might pertain. Then, having noted that, in order to know these proportions, I would sometimes need to consider each of them individually, and sometimes only to keep them in mind, or to grasp many of them together, I thought that, in order better to consider them in particular, I ought to suppose them to be relations between lines, since I found nothing more simple, or nothing that I could represent more distinctly to my imagination and to my senses; but that, in order to keep them in mind or to grasp many of them together, I would have to explicate them by means of certain symbols, the briefest ones possible; and that by this means I would be borrowing all that is best in geometrical analysis and algebra, and correcting all the defects of the one by means of the other.

In fact, I dare say the strict adherence to these few precepts I had chosen gave me such facility for disentangling all the questions to which these two sciences extend, that, in the two or three months I spent examining them, having begun with the simplest and most general, and each truth that I found being a rule that later helped me to find others, not only did I arrive at a solution of many problems that I had previously judged very difficult, but also it seemed to me toward the end that, even in those instances where I was ignorant, I could determine by what means and how far it was possible to resolve them. In this perhaps I shall not seem to you to be too vain, if you will consider that, there being but one truth with respect to each thing, whoever finds this truth knows as much about a thing as can be known; and that, for example, if a child who has been instructed in arithmetic has made an addition following its rules, he can be assured of having found everything regarding the sum he was examining that the human mind would know how to find. For ultimately, the method that teaches one to follow the true order and to enumerate exactly all the circumstances of what one is seeking contains everything that gives certainty to the rules of arithmetic.

But what pleased me most about this method was that by means of it I was assured of using my reason in everything, if not perfectly, at least as well as was in my power; and in addition that I felt that in practicing this method my mind was little by little getting into the habit of conceiving its objects more rigorously and more distinctly and that, not having restricted the method to any particular subject matter, I promised myself to apply it as usefully to the problems of the other sciences as I had to those of algebra. Not that, on this account, I would have dared at the outset to undertake an examination of all the problems that presented themselves, for that would itself have been contrary to the order prescribed by the method. But having noted that the principles of these sciences must all be derived from philosophy, in which I did not yet find any that were certain, I thought that it was necessary for me first of all to try to establish some there and that, this being the most important thing in the world, and the thing in which hasty judgment and prejudice were most to feared, I should not try to accomplish that objective until I had reached a much more mature age than that of merely twenty-three, which I was then, and until I had first spent a great deal of time preparing myself for it, as much in rooting out from my mind all the wrong opinions that I had accepted before that time as in accumulating many experiences, in order for them later to be the subject matter of my reasonings, and in always practicing the method I had prescribed for myself so as to strengthen myself more and more in its use.

Part Three

And finally, just as it is not enough, before beginning to rebuild the house where one is living, simply to pull it down, and to make provision for materials and architects or to train oneself in architecture, and also to have carefully drawn up the building plans for it; but it is also necessary to be provided with someplace else where one can live comfortably while working on it; so too, in order not to remain irresolute in my actions while reason required me to be so in my judgments, and in order not to cease to live as happily as possible during this time, I formulated a provisional code of morals, which consisted of but three or four maxims, which I very much want to share with you.

The first was to obey the laws and the customs of my country, constantly holding on to the religion in which, by God's grace, I had been instructed from my childhood, and governing myself in everything else according to the most moderate opinions and those furthest from excess—opinions that were commonly accepted in practice by the most judicious of those with whom I would have to live. For, beginning from then on to count my own opinions as nothing because I wished to submit them all to examination, I was assured that I could not do better than to follow those of the most judicious. And although there may perhaps be people among the Persians or the Chinese just as judicious as there are among ourselves, it seemed to me that the most useful thing was to rule myself in accordance with those with whom I had to live, and that, in order to know what their opinions truly were, I ought to pay attention to what they did rather than to what they said, not only because in the corruption of our morals there are few people who are willing to say everything they believe, but also because many do not know what they believe, for, given that the action of thought by which one believes something is different from that by which one knows that one believes it, the one often occurs without the other. And among many opinions that are equally accepted, I would choose only the most moderate, not only because they are always the most suitable for practical affairs and probably the best (every excess usually being bad), but also so as to stray less from the true path, in case I should be mistaken, than if I had chosen one of the two extremes when it was the other one I should have followed. And in particular I counted among the excesses all the promises by which one curtails something of one's freedom. Not that I disapproved of laws that, to remedy the inconstancy of weak minds, permit someone, when he has a good plan or even, for the security of commerce, some plan that is merely indifferent, to make vows or contracts that oblige him to persevere in it, but because I saw nothing in the world that always remained in the same state, and because, for my part, I promised myself to improve my judgments more and more, and never to make them worse, I would have thought I committed a grave indiscretion against good sense if, having once approved of something, I had obliged myself to take it as good again later, when perhaps it might have stopped being so or when I might have stopped considering it as such.

My second maxim was to be as firm and resolute in my actions as I could, and to follow the most doubtful opinions, once I had decided on them, with no less constancy than if they had been very well assured. In this I would be imitating travelers who, finding themselves lost in some forest, should not wander about turning this way and that, nor, worse still, stop in one place, but should always walk in as straight a line as they can in one direction and never change it for feeble reasons, even if at the outset it had perhaps been only chance that made them choose it, for by this means, even if they are not going exactly where they wish, at least they will eventually arrive somewhere where they will probably be better off than in the middle of a forest. And thus the actions of life often tolerating no delay, it is a very certain truth that, when it is not in our power to discern the truest opinions, we must follow the most probable, and even if we notice no more probability in some than in others, nevertheless we must settle on some, and afterwards no longer regard them as doubtful, insofar as they relate to practical matters, but as very true and very certain, because the reason that made us decide on them appears so. And from then on this was able to free me from all the regret and remorse that usually agitate the consciences of those frail and irresolute minds that allow themselves inconstantly to go about treating as if good things they later judge to be bad.

My third maxim was always to try to conquer myself rather than fortune, and to change my desires rather than the order of the world, and generally to accustom myself to believing that there is nothing that is completely within our power except our thoughts, so that, after we have done our best regarding things external to us, everything that is lacking for us to succeed is, from our point of view, absolutely impossible. And this alone seemed to me sufficient to prevent me in the future from desiring anything but what I was to acquire, and thus to make me contented. For, our will tending by nature to desire only what our understanding represents to it as somehow possible, it is certain that, if we consider all the goods that are outside us as equally beyond our power, we will have no more regrets about lacking those that seem owed to us as our birthright when we are deprived of them through no fault of our own, than we have in not possessing the kingdoms of China or Mexico, and that, making a virtue of necessity, as they say, we shall no more desire to be healthy if we are sick, or to be free if we are in prison, than we now do to have a body made of a material as incorruptible as diamonds, or wings to fly like birds. But I admit that long exercise is needed as well as frequently repeated meditation, in order to become accustomed to looking at everything from this point of view; and I believe that it is principally in this that the secret of those philosophers consists, who in earlier times were able to free themselves from fortune's domination and who, despite sorrows and poverty, could rival their gods in happiness. For occupying themselves ceaselessly with considering the limits prescribed to them by nature, they so perfectly persuaded themselves that nothing was in their power but their thoughts, that this alone was sufficient to prevent them from having any affection for other things, and they controlled their thoughts so absolutely that in this they had some reason for reckoning themselves richer, more powerful, freer, and happier than any other men who, not having this philosophy, never thus controlled everything they wished to control, however favored by nature and fortune they might be.

    Finally, to conclude this code of morals, I took it upon myself to review the various occupations that men have in this life, in order to try to choose the best one, and, not wanting to say anything about the occupations of others, I thought I could not do better than to continue in that very one in which I found myself, that is to say, spending my whole life cultivating my reason and advancing, as far as I could, in the knowledge of the truth, following the method I had prescribed to myself. I had met with such extreme contentment since the time I had begun to make use of this method, that I did not believe one could obtain any sweeter or more innocent contentment in this life, and, discovering every day by its means some truths that to me seemed quite important and commonly ignored by other men, the satisfaction I had from them so filled my mind that nothing else was of any consequence to me. In addition, the three preceding maxims were founded solely on the plan I had of continuing to instruct myself, for since God has given each of us some light to distinguish the true from the false, I would not have believed I ought to rest content for a single moment with the opinions of others, had I not proposed to use my own judgment to examine them when there would be time; and I would not have been able to free myself of scruples in following these opinions, had I not hoped that I would not, on that account, lose any opportunity of finding better ones, in case there were any. And finally, I could not have limited my desires or have been content, had I not followed a path by which, thinking I was assured of acquiring all the knowledge of which I was capable, I thought I was assured by the same means of the knowledge of all the true goods that would ever be in my power. For, given that our will tends not to pursue or flee anything unless our understanding represents it to the will as either good or bad, it suffices to judge well in order to do well, and to judge as best one can, in order also to do one's very best, that is to say, to acquire all the virtues and in general all the other goods that one could acquire, and, when one is certain that this is the case, one could not fail to be contented.

When I had thus assured myself of these maxims and put them to one side along with the truths of the faith, which have always held first place among my beliefs, I judged that, as for the rest of my opinions, I could freely undertake to rid myself of them. And inasmuch as I hoped to be able to reach my goal better by conversing with men than by staying shut up any longer in the stove-heated room[5] where I had had all these thoughts, the winter was not yet over when I set out again on my travels. And in all the nine years that followed I did nothing but wander here and there in the world, trying to be more a spectator than an actor in all the comedies that are played out there; and reflecting particularly in each matter on what might render it suspect and give us occasion for erring, I meanwhile rooted out from my mind all the errors that had previously been able to slip into it. Not that, in order to do this, I was imitating the skeptics who doubt merely for the sake of doubting and put on the affectation of being perpetually undecided, for, on the contrary, my entire plan tended simply to give me assurance and to cast aside the shifting earth and sand in order to find rock or clay. In this I was quite successful, it seems to me, inasmuch as, trying to discover the falsity or the uncertainty of the propositions I was examining, not by feeble conjectures but by clear and certain reasonings, I never found any that was so doubtful that I could not draw from it some quite certain conclusion, even if it had been merely that it contained nothing certain. And just as in tearing down an old house, one usually

---

5. See f.n. 3, p. 7.

saves the wreckage for use in building a new one, similarly, in destroying all those opinions of mine that I judged to be poorly founded, I made various observations and acquired many experiences that have since served me in establishing more certain opinions. Moreover, I continued to practice the method I had prescribed for myself, for, besides taking care generally to conduct all my thoughts according to its rules, from time to time I set aside some hours that I spent particularly in applying it to mathematical problems, or even also to some other problems that I could make as it were similar to those of mathematics, by detaching them from all the principles of the other sciences, which I did not find to be sufficiently firm, as you will see I have done in many problems that are explained in this volume.[6] And thus, without living any differently in outward appearance than do those who, having no task but to live a sweet and innocent life, make a point of separating pleasures from vices, and who, in order to enjoy their leisure without becoming bored, involve themselves in all sorts of honest diversions, I did not cease to carry out my plan and to progress in the knowledge of the truth, perhaps more than if I had done nothing but read books or keep company with men of letters.

Nevertheless, those nine years slipped by before I had as yet taken any stand regarding the difficulties commonly debated among learned men, or had begun to seek the foundations of any philosophy that was more certain than the commonly accepted one. And the example of many excellent minds, who had previously had this plan and had not, it seemed to me, succeeded in it, made me imagine so much difficulty in it that perhaps I would not have dared to undertake it so soon again, if I had not seen that some had already spread the rumor that I had achieved my goal. I cannot say on what they based this opinion, and if I have contributed something to it by my conversation, this must have been because I confessed that of which I was ignorant more ingenuously than those who have studied only a little are in the habit of doing, and perhaps also because I showed the reasons I had for doubting many things that other people regard as certain, rather than because I was boasting of any learning. But having a good enough heart not to want someone to take me for something other than I was, I thought it necessary to try by every means to render myself worthy of the reputation that was bestowed on me. And it is exactly eight years ago that this desire made me resolve to take my leave of all those places where I might have acquaintances, and to retire here, to a country where the long duration of the war has led to the establishment of such well-ordered discipline that the armies quartered here seem to serve only to make one enjoy the fruits of peace with even

---

6. Descartes also published treatises on optics, geometry, and meteorology in this same volume.

greater security, and where, in the midst of the crowd of a great and very busy people who are more concerned with their own affairs than they are curious about those of others, I have been able, without lacking any of the amenities to be found in the most bustling cities, to live as solitary and as withdrawn a life as I could in the remotest deserts.

Part Four

I do not know whether I ought to tell you about the first meditations I engaged in there, for they are so metaphysical and so out of the ordinary that perhaps they will not be to everyone's liking. And yet, in order that it should be possible to judge whether the foundations I have laid are sufficiently firm, I find myself in some sense forced to talk about them. For a long time I had noticed that in matters of morality one must sometimes follow opinions that one knows to be quite uncertain, just as if they were indubitable, as has been said above, but because I then desired to devote myself exclusively to the search for the truth, I thought it necessary that I do exactly the opposite, and that I reject as absolutely false everything in which I could imagine the least doubt, in order to see whether, after this process, something in my beliefs remained that was entirely indubitable. Thus, because our senses sometimes deceive us, I wanted to suppose that nothing was exactly as they led us to imagine. And because there are men who make mistakes in reasoning, even in the simplest matters in geometry, and who commit paralogisms, judging that I was just as prone to err as any other, I rejected as false all the reasonings that I had previously taken for demonstrations. And finally, considering the fact that all the same thoughts we have when we are awake can also come to us when we are asleep, without any of them being true, I resolved to pretend that all the things that had ever entered my mind were no more true than the illusions of my dreams. But immediately afterward I noticed that, while I wanted thus to think that everything was false, it necessarily had to be the case that I, who was thinking this, was something. And noticing that this truth—*I think, therefore I am*—was so firm and so assured that all the most extravagant suppositions of the skeptics were incapable of shaking it, I judged that I could accept it without scruple as the first principle of the philosophy I was seeking.

Then, examining with attention what I was, and seeing that I could pretend that I had no body and that there was no world nor any place where I was, I could not pretend, on that account, that I did not exist at all, and that, on the contrary, from the very fact that I thought of doubting the truth of other things, it followed very evidently and very certainly that I existed; whereas, on the other hand, had I simply stopped thinking, even if all the rest of what I had ever imagined had been true, I would have had no reason to believe that I had existed. From this I knew that I was a substance the whole essence or nature of which is simply to think, and which, in order to exist, has no need of any place nor depends on any material thing. Thus this "I," that is to say, the soul through which I am what I am, is entirely distinct from the body and is even easier to know than the body, and even if there were no body at all, it would not cease to be all that it is.

After this, I considered in general what is needed for a proposition to be true and certain, for since I had just found one of them that I knew to be such, I thought I ought also to know in what this certitude consists. And having noticed that there is nothing at all in this *I think, therefore I am* that assures me that I am speaking the truth, except that I see very clearly that, in order to think, it is necessary to exist, I judged that I could take as a general rule that the things we conceive very clearly and very distinctly are all true, but that there is merely some difficulty in properly discerning which are those that we distinctly conceive.

Following this, reflecting upon the fact that I doubted and that, as a consequence, my being was not utterly perfect (for I saw clearly that it is a greater perfection to know than to doubt), I decided to search for the source from which I had learned to think of something more perfect than I was, and I plainly knew that this had to be from some nature that was in fact more perfect. As to those thoughts I had of many other things outside me, such as the heavens, the earth, light, heat, and a thousand others, I had no trouble at all knowing where they came from, because, noticing nothing in them that seemed to me to make them superior to me, I could believe that, if they were true, they were dependencies of my nature, insofar as it had some perfection, and that, if they were not true, I obtained them from nothing, that is to say, they were in me because I had some defect. But the same could not hold for the idea of a being more perfect than my own, for it is a manifest contradiction to receive this idea from nothing, and because it is no less a contradiction that something more perfect should follow from and depend upon something less perfect than that something should come from nothing, I could not obtain it from myself. It thus remained that this idea had been placed in me by a nature truly more perfect than I was and that it even had within itself all the perfections of which I could have any idea, that is to say, to explain myself in a single word, that it was God. To this I added that, since I knew of some perfections that I did not at all possess, I was not the only being that existed (here, if you please, I shall freely use the terminology of the School), but that of necessity there must be something else more perfect, upon which I depended, and from which I had acquired all that I had. For, had I been alone and independent of everything else, so that I had had from myself all that small amount of perfection in which I participated in the perfect being, I would have been able, for the same reason, to have from myself everything else I knew I lacked, and thus to be myself infinite, eternal, unchanging, all-knowing, all-powerful; in short, to have all the perfections I could observe to be in God. For, following the reasonings I have just gone through, in order to know the nature of God, so far as my own nature was capable of doing so, I had only to consider, regarding all the things of which I found in myself some idea, whether or not it was a perfection to possess them, and I was assured that none of those that indicated any imperfection were in God, but that all others were in him. Thus I saw that doubt, inconstancy, sadness, and the like could not be in God, since I myself would have been happy to be exempt from them. Then, besides this, I had ideas of a number of sensible and corporeal things, for even if I were to suppose that I was dreaming and that everything I saw or imagined was false, I still could not deny that the ideas of these things were truly in my thought. But since I had already recognized very clearly in myself that intelligent nature is distinct from corporeal nature, taking into consideration that all composition attests to dependence and that dependence is manifestly a defect, I judged from this that being composed of these two natures could not be a perfection in God and that, as a consequence, God was not thus composed, but that, if there are bodies in the world, or even intelligences, or other natures that were not at all entirely perfect, their being had to depend on God's power in such wise that they could not subsist without God for a single moment.

After this, I wanted to search for other truths, and, having set before myself the object dealt with by geometers, which I conceived of as a continuous body or a space indefinitely extended in length, breadth, and height or depth, divisible into various parts which could have various shapes and sizes and which may be moved or transposed in all sorts of ways—for the geometers assume all this in their object—I went through some of their simplest demonstrations. And, having noted that the great certitude that everyone attributes to these demonstrations is founded exclusively on the fact that they are plainly conceived, following the rule that I mentioned earlier, I also noted that there was nothing at all in them that assured me of the existence of their object. For I saw very well that if one supposed, for example, a triangle, it was necessary for its three angles to be equal to two right angles, but I did not see anything in all this to assure me that there was any triangle existing in the world. On the other hand, returning to examine the idea I had of a perfect being, I found that existence was contained in it in the same way in which the equality of its three angles to two right angles is contained in the idea of a triangle, or that the equidistance of all its parts from its center is contained in the idea of a sphere, or even more plainly still, and that, consequently, it is, at the very least, just as certain that God, who is this perfect being, is or exists, as any demonstration in geometry could be.

But what brings it about that there are many people who are persuaded that it is difficult to know this and also even to know what their soul is is that they never lift their minds above sensible things and that they are so accustomed to consider nothing except by imagining it (which is a way of thinking appropriate for material things), that everything unimaginable seems to them unintelligible. This is obvious enough from the fact that even philosophers take it as a maxim in the schools that there is nothing in the understanding that has not first been in the senses, where it is nevertheless certain that the ideas of God and the soul have never been. And it seems to me that those who want to use their imagination in order to grasp these ideas are doing the very same thing as if, in order to hear sounds or to smell odors, they wanted to use their eyes. There is just this difference: the sense of sight assures us no less of the truth of its objects than do the senses of smell or hearing, whereas neither our imagination nor our senses could ever assure us of anything if our understanding did not intervene.

Finally, if there still are men who have not been sufficiently persuaded of the existence of God and of their soul by means of the reasons I have brought forward, I very much want them to know that all the other things of which they think themselves perhaps more assured, such as having a body, that there are stars and an earth, and the like, are less certain. For although one might have a moral assurance about these things, which is such that it seems one cannot doubt them without being extravagant, still when it is a question of metaphysical certitude, it seems unreasonable for anyone to deny that there is not a sufficient basis for one's being completely assured about them, when one observes that while asleep one can, in the same fashion, imagine that one has a different body and that one sees different stars and a different earth, without any of these things being the case. For how does one know that the thoughts that come to us in dreams are any more false than the others, given that they are often no less vivid and explicit? And even if the best minds study this as much as they please, I do not believe they can give any reason sufficient to remove this doubt, unless they presuppose the existence of God. For first of all, even what I have already taken for a rule, namely that the things we very clearly and very distinctly conceive are all true, is assured only for the reason that God is or exists, and that he is a perfect being, and that all that is in us comes from him. It follows from this that our ideas or notions, being real things and coming from God, cannot, in all that is clear and distinct in them, be anything but true. Thus, if we quite often have ideas that contain some falsity, this can only be the case with respect to things that have something confused or obscure about them, because in this respect they participate in nothing; that is, they are thus confused in us only because we are not perfect. And it is evident that it is no less a contradiction that falsity or imperfection as such proceeds from God, than that truth or perfection proceeds from nothing. But if we did not know that all that is real and true in us comes from a perfect and infinite being, however clear and distinct our ideas were, we would have no reason that assured us that they had the perfection of being true.

But once the knowledge of God and the soul has thus made us certain of this rule, it is very easy to know that the dreams we imagine while asleep ought in no way to make us doubt the truth of the thoughts we have while awake. For if it did happen, even while asleep, that one had a very distinct idea (as, for example, if a geometer found some new demonstration), one's being asleep would not prevent its being true. And as to the most common error of our dreams, which consists in the fact that they represent to us various objects in the same way as our external senses do, it does not matter that it gives us occasion to question the truth of such ideas, since they can also deceive us quite often without our being asleep, such as when those with jaundice see everything as yellow, or when the stars or other very distant bodies appear to us much smaller than they are. For finally, whether awake or asleep, we should never allow ourselves to be persuaded except by the evidence of our reason. And it is to be observed that I say "of our reason," and not "of our imagination" or "of our senses." Even though we see the sun very clearly, we should not on that account judge that it is only as large as we see it, and we can well imagine distinctly the head of a lion grafted onto the body of a goat, without having to conclude for that reason that there is a chimera in the world, for reason does not at all dictate to us that what we thus see or imagine is true. But it does dictate to us that all our ideas or notions must have some foundation of truth, for it would not be possible that God, who is all-perfect and all-truthful, would have put them in us without that. And because our reasonings are never so evident nor so complete while we are asleep as they are while we are awake, even though our imaginings while we are asleep are sometimes just as vivid and explicit as those we have while we are awake, or even more so, reason also dictates to us that our thoughts cannot all be true, since we are not all-perfect; what truth there is in them must infallibly be encountered in those we have when we are awake rather than in those we have in our dreams.

Part Five

I would be quite happy to continue and to show here the whole chain of other truths that I have deduced from these first ones. But because, in order to do this, it would now be necessary for me to speak about many questions that are a matter of controversy among the learned, with whom I have no desire to get into any quarrel, I believe it will be better for me to abstain from this and to state only in a general way what these questions are, in order to let those who are wiser judge whether it would be useful for the public to be more particularly informed about them. I have always remained firm in the resolution I had made not to suppose any principle but the one I have just used to demonstrate the existence of God and of the soul, and not to accept anything as true that did not seem to me clearer and more certain than the demonstrations of the geometers had hitherto seemed. And, nevertheless, I dare say not only that have I found a means of satisfying myself within a short time regarding all the principal difficulties commonly treated in philosophy, but also that I have noted certain laws that God has so established in nature, and of which he has impressed in our souls such notions, that, after having reflected sufficiently on these matters, we cannot doubt that they are strictly adhered to in everything that exists or occurs in the world. Moreover, in considering the consequences of these laws, it seems to me that I have discovered many truths more useful and more important than all that I had previously learned or even hoped to learn.

But because I have tried to explain the principal ones among these truths in a treatise that certain considerations prevented me from publishing,[7] I could not make them better known than by stating here in summary form what the treatise contains. I had intended to include in it everything that I thought I knew, before writing it down, concerning the nature of material things. But just as painters, who are unable to represent equally well on a flat surface all the various sides of a solid body, choose one of the principal sides which they place alone facing the light of day, and, by darkening the rest with shadows, make them appear only as they can be seen by someone who is looking at the principal side, just so, fearing I could not put into my discourse everything I had in mind about it, I undertook in it merely to speak at length about what I conceived with respect to light; then, at the proper time, to add something about the sun and the fixed stars, because light proceeds almost entirely from them;

---

7. Descartes' *Le Monde* (*The World*). See René Descartes, *Le Monde ou Traité de la lumière*, translation and introduction by Michael Sean Mahoney (New York: Abaris Books, Inc., 1979). One of the considerations preventing the publication of *Le Monde* was the trial in 1633 of Galileo by the Holy Office in Rome.

something about the heavens, because they transmit light; about planets, comets, and the earth, because they reflect light; and, in particular, about all terrestrial bodies, because they are either colored, or transparent, or luminous; and finally, about man, because he is the observer of these things. All the same, to cast all these things a little in shadow and to be able to say more freely what I judged about them without being obliged either to follow or to refute the opinions that are accepted among the learned, I resolved to leave this entire world here to their disputes, and to speak only of what would happen in a new world, were God now to create enough matter to compose it, somewhere in imaginary spaces, and were he to agitate in various ways and without order the different parts of this matter, so that he composed from it a chaos as confused as any the poets could concoct and that later he did no more than apply his ordinary concurrence to nature, and let nature act in accordance with the laws he had established. Thus, first, I described this matter and tried to represent it in such a way that there is nothing in the world, it seems to me, clearer and more intelligible, with the exception of what has already been said about God and the soul, for I even explicitly supposed that in this matter there were none of those forms or qualities about which disputes occur in the schools, nor generally anything the knowledge of which was not so natural to our souls that one could not even pretend to be ignorant of it. Moreover, I showed what the laws of nature were, and, without supporting my reasons on any other principle but the infinite perfections of God, I tried to demonstrate all those laws about which one might have been able to have any doubt and to show that they are such that, even if God had created many worlds, there could not be any of them in which these laws failed to be observed. After that, I showed how, as a consequence of these laws, the greater part of the matter of this chaos had to be disposed and arranged in a certain way, which made it similar to our heavens; how, at the same time, some of its parts had to compose an earth; others, planets and comets; and still others, a sun and fixed stars. And here, dwelling on the subject of light, I explained at some length what this light was that had to be found in the sun and the stars, and how from thence it travelled in an instant across the immense spaces of the heavens, and how it was reflected from the planets and comets to the earth. To this I added also a number of things touching on the substance, position, motions, and all the various qualities of these heavens and these stars; and as a result, I thought I said enough on these matters to show that there is nothing to be observed in the things of this world which should not, or at least could not, have appeared entirely similar in those of the world I was describing. From there, I went on to speak in particular about the earth: how, although I had expressly supposed that

God had not put any weight[8] in the matter out of which the earth was composed, none of its parts ceased to tend precisely toward its center; how, there being water and air on its surface, the disposition of the heavens and of the stars, principally of the moon, had to cause there an ebb and flow similar in all respects to what we observe in our seas, and, in addition, a certain coursing, as much of the water as of the air, from east to west, such as is also observed between the tropics; how mountains, seas, springs, and rivers could naturally be formed there, and how metals could make their way into mines there; how plants could grow naturally in the fields there, and generally how all the bodies called "mixed" or "composed" could be engendered there. And, among other things, because apart from the stars I know of nothing else in the world that would produce light except fire, I tried to make very clearly understood all that belonged to its nature: how it is made, how it is nourished, how sometimes it has only heat but no light, and sometimes only light but no heat; how it can introduce various colors and various other qualities into various bodies; how it melts some bodies and hardens others; how it can consume nearly all of them or turn them into ashes and smoke; and finally, how from these ashes, merely by the force of its action, it produces glass, for since this transmutation of ashes into glass seemed to me to be as awesome as any other that occurs in nature, I took particular pleasure in describing it.

Yet I did not want to infer from all these things that this world has been created in the manner I was proposing, for it is much more likely that, from the beginning, God made it such as it had to be. But it is certain (and this is an opinion commonly accepted among theologians) that the action by which God preserves the world is precisely the same as that by which he created it; so that, even if, in the beginning, he had never given it any other form at all but that of a chaos, provided he established the laws of nature and bestowed his concurrence in order for nature to function just as it does ordinarily, one can believe, without doing injustice to the miracle of creation, that by this means alone all the things that are purely material could over time have been rendered such as we now see them. And their nature is much easier to conceive, when one sees them coming to be little by little in this manner, than when one considers them only in their completed state.

From the description of inanimate bodies and plants I passed to that of animals and in particular to that of human beings. But because I did

---

8. E. Gilson, in his *Discours de la méthode: texte et commentaire*, p. 388, observes that *pesanteur* here means the same thing as *gravitas*, a scholastic term referring to the tendency of terrestrial objects always to tend downwards. Gilson also directs the reader to *The World*, chapter xi: "On Weight."

not yet have sufficient knowledge of them to speak of them in the same manner as I did of the rest, that is to say, by demonstrating effects from causes and by showing from what seeds and in what manner nature must produce them, I contented myself with supposing that God formed the body of a man exactly like one of ours, as much in the outward shape of its members as in the internal arrangement of its organs, without composing it out of any material but the type I had described, and without putting into it, at the start, any rational soul, or anything else to serve there as a vegetative or sensitive soul, but merely kindled in the man's heart one of those fires without light which I had already explained and which I did not at all conceive to be of a nature other than what heats hay when it has been stored before it is dry, or which makes new wines boil when they are left to ferment after crushing. For on examining the functions that could, as a consequence, be in this body, I found there precisely all those things that can be in us without our thinking about them, and hence, without our soul's contributing to them, that is to say, that part distinct from the body of which it has been said previously that its nature is only to think. And these are all the same features in which one can say that animals lacking reason resemble us. But I could not on that account find there any of those functions, which, being dependent on thought, are the only ones that belong to us as men, although I did find them all later on, once I had supposed that God created a rational soul and joined it to this body in a particular manner that I described.

But in order that one might be able to see how I treated this matter there, I want to place here the explanation of the movement of the heart and of the arteries, because, this being the first and most general movement that one observes in animals, on the basis of it one will easily judge what one ought to think about all the others. And, in order that there might be less difficulty in understanding what I shall say on the matter, I would like those who are not at all versed in anatomy to take the trouble, before reading this, to have the heart of some large animal that has lungs dissected in their presence (for such a heart is in all respects sufficiently similar to that of a man), and to be shown the two chambers or cavities that are in it. First, there is the one on the right side of the heart, into which two very large tubes lead, namely the *vena cava,* which is the principal receptacle of the blood, and which is like the trunk of a tree of which the other veins of the body are the branches, and the arterial vein (which has thus been rather ill-named, because it is, in effect, an artery), which, taking its origin from the heart, divides up after leaving the heart into many branches that go on to be spread throughout the lungs. Then there is the chamber or cavity on the left side, into which two tubes lead in the same fashion, which are as large as or larger than the preceding ones: namely, the venous artery (which has also been ill-named, since it is nothing but a vein), which comes from the lungs, where it is divided into many branches interlaced with those of the arterial vein and with those in the passageway called the windpipe, through which the air one breathes enters, and the great artery, which, on leaving the heart, sends its branches throughout the body. I would also like those who are not versed in anatomy to be carefully shown the eleven little membranes that, like so many little doors, open and shut the four openings in the two cavities: namely, three at the entrance to the *vena cava,* where they are so disposed that they cannot in any way prevent the blood it contains from flowing into the right cavity of the heart, and yet completely prevent it from being able to leave it: three at the entrance to the arterial vein, which, being arranged totally in the other direction, readily permit the blood in this cavity to pass into the lungs, but do not permit any blood in the lungs to return there; likewise, two others at the entrance to the venous artery, which let blood flow from the lungs into the left cavity of the heart but block its return; and three at the entrance to the great artery, which permit blood to leave the heart but prevent it from returning there. And there is no need at all to search for any other reason for the number of membranes except that the opening of the venous artery, being oval-shaped because of its location, can conveniently be closed with two, while the other openings, being round, can better be closed with three. Further, I would like to make them consider that the great artery and the arterial vein are of a much harder and firmer constitution than the venous artery and the *vena cava,* and that these latter two become enlarged before entering the heart and there form, as it were, sacks, called the "auricles" of the heart, which are made of flesh similar to that of the heart; and that there is always more heat in the heart than anywhere else in the body, and, finally, that this heat is able to bring it about that, if a drop of blood enters its cavities, it promptly expands and is dilated, just as all liquids generally do when one lets them fall drop by drop into some vessel that is very hot.

For, after that, I have no need to say anything else in order to explain the movement of the heart, except that, when its cavities are not full of blood, blood necessarily flows from the *vena cava* into the right cavity and from the venous artery into the left cavity, given that these two vessels are always full of blood, and their openings, which face the heart, cannot then be closed. But as soon as two drops of blood have thus entered the heart, one into each of its cavities, these drops, which can only be very large because the openings through which they enter are very wide and the vessels from whence they come are quite full of blood, are rarified and dilated because of the heat they find there, by means of which, making the whole heart inflate, they push and close the five little doors that are at the entrances to the two vessels from whence they come, thus preventing any more blood from descending into the heart, and, continuing to become more and more rarified, they push and open the six other little doors which are at the entrances to the other two vessels by which they leave. By this means they inflate all the branches of the arterial vein and the great artery, almost at the same instant as the heart; immediately afterward the heart contracts, as do these arteries as well, because the blood that has entered them gets cooled and their six little doors close again, and the five doors of the *vena cava* and the venous artery reopen and grant passage to two other drops of blood, which immediately make the heart and the arteries inflate exactly as before. And, because the blood that thus enters the heart passes through the two sacks called its auricles, it follows from this that their movement is contrary to that of the heart, and that they are deflated while the heart is inflated. As for the rest (in order that those who do not know the force of mathematical demonstrations and are not accustomed to distinguishing true reasons from probable ones should not venture to deny this without examining it), I want to put them on notice that this movement which I have just been explaining follows just as necessarily from the mere disposition of the organs that can be seen in the heart by the naked eye, and from the heat that can be felt with the fingers, and from the nature of blood, which can be known through observation, as does the movement of a clock from the force, placement, and shape of its counterweights and wheels.

But if one asks how it is that the blood in the veins is not at all dissipated in flowing thus continually into the heart, and how the arteries are never overly full of blood, since all the blood that flows through the heart is going to flow into them, to this I need give no other answer than what has already been written by an English physician,[9] to whom homage must be paid for having broken the ice in this area, and for being the first to have taught that there are many small passages at the extremities of the arteries through which the blood they receive enters into the small branches of the veins, from which it flows immediately to the heart, so that its course is merely a perpetual circulation. He proves this very effectively from the common experience of surgeons, who, on binding an arm moderately tightly above the spot where they open the vein, cause the blood to flow out in even greater abundance than if they had not bound the arm at all. And just the opposite would happen if they bound the arm below,

---

9. William Harvey (1578–1657), English physiologist who demonstrated the function of the heart and the complete circulation of blood throughout the body. His most important work is *Anatomical Exercises on the Motion of the Heart and Blood* (1628). Descartes accepted Harvey's account of how blood circulated, but not his account of the heart's motion.

between the hand and the opening, or even if they bind it very tightly above the opening, for it is obvious that a moderately tight tourniquet, being able to prevent the blood that is already in the arm from returning to the heart through the veins, does not on that account prevent new blood from coming in through the arteries, because they are located below the veins, and their membranes, being harder, are less easy to press, and also because the blood coming from the heart tends to pass through the arteries toward the hand with greater force than it does in returning from these to the heart through the veins. And since this blood leaves the arm through the opening in one of the veins, there must necessarily be some passages below the tourniquet, that is to say, toward the extremities of the arm, through which it could come from the arteries. He also proves quite effectively what he says regarding the circulation of blood by referring to certain small membranes that are so disposed in various places along the length of the veins that they do not at all permit blood to pass from the middle of the body toward the extremities, but only to return from the extremities toward the heart; and further, by means of the experiment that shows that all the blood that is in the body can flow out of it in a very short time through just one artery when it is cut open, even if the artery is very tightly bound quite close to the heart, and cut open between the heart and the tourniquet, so that one would have no basis for imagining that the blood that flowed out came from somewhere else.

But there are many other things that attest to the fact that the true cause of this movement of blood is as I have said. First, the difference that one notices between the blood leaving the veins and the blood leaving the arteries can result only from the fact that the blood is rarified and, as it were, distilled, in passing through the heart; it is thinner, livelier, and warmer just after having left the heart, that is to say, while it is in the arteries, than it is shortly before it enters the heart, that is to say, while it is in the veins. And if one takes note of it, one will find that this difference is more readily apparent near the heart and not at all so much in those places furthest removed from the heart. Then the hardness of the membranes of which the arterial vein and the great artery are composed shows well enough that the blood beats against them with more force than it does against the veins. And why would the left cavity of the heart and the great artery be larger and wider than the right cavity and the arterial vein, unless it is because the blood in the venous artery, having been only in the lungs after having passed through the heart, is thinner and is more forcefully and more easily rarified than what comes immediately from the *vena cava*? And what can physicians divine from taking the pulse, if they do not know that, as the blood changes its nature, it can be rarified by the heat of the heart more or less strongly, and more

52

or less quickly than before? And if one examines how this heat is communicated to the other members, must one not admit that it is by means of the blood, which, on passing through the heart, is reheated there and from there is spread throughout the whole body? It follows from this that if one removes the blood from some part of the body, one thereupon also removes the heat; and even if the heart were as hot as a piece of glowing iron, it would not be enough to reheat the feet and hands as much as it does, if it did not continuously send new blood to them. Then, too, it is also evident from this that the true function of respiration is to bring enough fresh air into the lungs to cause the blood which comes there from the right cavity of the heart, where it has been rarified and, as it were, changed into vapors, immediately to be condensed and to be converted once again into blood before returning to the left cavity; without this process the blood could not properly aid in feeding the fire that is in the heart. This is confirmed because one sees that animals without lungs have but one single cavity in their hearts, and that children, who cannot use their lungs while enclosed within their mother's womb, have an opening through which blood flows from the *vena cava* into the left cavity of the heart, as well as a tube through which blood goes from the arterial vein to the great artery without passing through the lungs. Next, how would digestion take place in the stomach if the heart did not send heat there through the arteries, and with it some of the most fluid parts of the blood, which help dissolve the food that has gone there? And is it not easy to understand the action that changes the juice of this food into blood, if one considers that, in passing and repassing through the heart, it is distilled perhaps more than one or two hundred times a day? And is anything else needed to explain nutrition and the production of the various humors that are in the body, except to say that the force with which the blood, in being rarified, passes from the heart toward the extremities of the arteries, makes some of its parts stop in those parts of the members where they are found and there take the place of others that they expel from there; and that, according to the situation or the shape or the smallness of the pores they encounter, some of the parts of the blood tend to go certain places rather than others, in just the same way that anyone can have seen various sieves of different fineness serve to separate out different grains from one another? And finally what is most remarkable in all this is the generation of the animal spirits, which are like a very subtle wind, or rather, like a very pure and lively flame that rises continuously in great abundance from the heart to the brain, and from there goes through the nerves into the muscles, and gives movement to all the members. The parts of the blood that are the most agitated and penetrating, and are thus the best suited to compose these spirits, are going to move toward the brain rather than elsewhere; and there is no need to imagine any reason for this other than that the arteries that carry these parts of the blood there are those that come from the heart in the straightest line of all, and that, according to the laws of mechanics (which are the same as those of nature), when a number of things tend to move together in the same direction, where there is not enough room for all of them, as when the parts of the blood leaving the left cavity of the heart tend toward the brain, the weakest and least agitated must be pushed aside by the strongest which by this means arrive there alone.

I had provided a sufficiently detailed explanation for all these things in the treatise that I had previously intended to publish. And then I had shown what the constitution of the nerves and muscles of the human body must be in order to make the animal spirits within them have the force to move its members, as when one observes that heads, shortly after being severed, still move about and bite the earth, even though they are no longer alive. I had also shown what changes must take place in the brain in order to cause wakefulness, sleep, and dreams; how light, sounds, odors, tastes, heat, and all the other qualities of external objects can imprint various ideas there through the mediation of the senses; how hunger, thirst, and the other internal passions can also send their ideas there; what part of them needs to be taken there for the common sense, where these ideas are received, for the memory, which preserves them, and for the imagination, which can change them in various ways and compose new ones out of them, and, by the same means, distributing the animal spirits into the muscles, make the members of this body move in as many different ways (and in a manner appropriate to the objects that present themselves to the senses and to the internal passions that are in the body), as our own bodies can, without their being guided by the will. This will in no way seem strange to those who are cognizant of how many different automata or moving machines the ingenuity of men can make, without, in doing so, using more than a very small number of parts, in comparison with the great multitude of bones, muscles, nerves, arteries, veins, and all the other parts which are in the body of each animal. For they will regard this body as a machine which, having been made by the hands of God, is incomparably better ordered and has within itself movements far more wondrous than any of those that can be invented by men.

And I paused here in particular in order to show that, if there were such machines having the organs and the shape of a monkey or of some other animal that lacked reason, we would have no way of recognizing that they were not entirely of the same nature as these animals; whereas, if there were any such machines that bore a resemblance to our bodies and imitated our actions as far as this is practically feasible, we would always have two very certain means of recognizing that they were not at all, for that reason, true men. The first is that they could never use words or other signs, or put them together as we do in order to declare our thoughts to others. For one can well conceive of a machine being so made that it utters words, and even that it utters words appropriate to the bodily actions that will cause some change in its organs (such as, if one touches it in a certain place, it asks what one wants to say to it, or, if in another place, it cries out that one is hurting it, and the like). But it could not arrange its words differently so as to respond to the sense of all that will be said in its presence, as even the dullest men can do. The second means is that, although they might perform many tasks very well or perhaps better than any of us, such machines would inevitably fail in other tasks; by this means one would discover that they were acting not through knowledge but only through the disposition of their organs. For while reason is a universal instrument that can be of help in all sorts of circumstances, these organs require some particular disposition for each particular action; consequently, it is for all practical purposes impossible for there to be enough different organs in a machine to make it act in all the contingencies of life in the same way as our reason makes us act.

Now by these two means one can also know the difference between men and beasts. For it is rather remarkable that there are no men so dull and so stupid (excluding not even the insane), that they are incapable of arranging various words together and of composing from them a discourse by means of which they might make their thoughts understood, and that, on the other hand, there is no other animal at all, however perfect and pedigreed it may be, that does the like. This does not happen because they lack the organs, for one sees that magpies and parrots can utter words just as we can, and yet they cannot speak as we do, that is to say, by testifying to the fact that they are thinking about what they are saying; on the other hand, men born deaf and dumb, who are deprived of the organs that aid others in speaking just as much as, or more than beasts, are wont to invent for themselves various signs by means of which they make themselves understood to those who, being with them on a regular basis, have the time to learn their language. And this attests not merely to the fact that beasts have less reason than men but that they have none at all. For it is obvious it does not need much to know how to speak; and since we notice as much inequality among animals of the same species as among men, and that some are easier to train than others, it is unbelievable that a monkey or a parrot that is the most perfect of its species would not equal in this respect one of the most stupid children or at least a child with a disordered brain, if their soul were not of a nature entirely different from our own. And we should not confuse words with the natural movements that attest to the passions and can be imitated by machines as well as by animals. Nor should we think, as did some of the ancients, that beasts speak, although we do not understand their language, for if that were true, since they have many organs corresponding to our own, they could make themselves as well understood by us as they are by their fellow creatures. It is also a very remarkable phenomenon that, although there are many animals that show more skill than we do in some of their actions, we nevertheless see that they show none at all in many other actions. Consequently, the fact that they do something better than we do does not prove that they have any intelligence, for, were that the case, they would have more of it than any of us and would excel us in everything. But rather it proves that they have no intelligence at all, and that it is nature that acts in them, according to the disposition of their organs—just as we see that a clock composed exclusively of wheels and springs can count the hours and measure time more accurately than we can with all our carefulness.

After that, I described the rational soul and showed that it can in no way be derived from the potentiality of matter, as can the other things I have spoken of, but rather that it must be expressly created; and how it is not enough for it to be lodged in the human body like a pilot in his ship, unless perhaps in order to move its members, but rather that it must be more closely joined and united to the body in order to have, in addition to this, feelings and appetites similar to our own, and thus to constitute a true man. As to the rest, I elaborated here a little on the subject of the soul because it is of the greatest importance; for, after the error of those who deny the existence of God (which I think I have sufficiently refuted), there is none at all that puts weak minds at a greater distance from the straight path of virtue than to imagine that the soul of beasts is of the same nature as ours, and that, as a consequence, we have nothing to fear or to hope for after this life any more than do flies and ants. On the other hand, when one knows how different they are, one understands much better the arguments which prove that our soul is of a nature entirely independent of the body, and consequently that it is not subject to die with it. Then, since we do not see any other causes at all for its destruction, we are naturally led to judge from this that it is immortal.

Part Six

But it is now three years since I arrived at the end of the treatise that contains all these things and began to review it in order to put it into the hands of a printer, when I learned that some people to whom I defer and whose authority over my actions can hardly be less than that of my reason over my thoughts, had disapproved of an opinion in physics, published a short time earlier by someone else,[10] concerning which I do not want to say that I was in agreement, but rather that I had not noticed anything in it, before their censuring of it, that I could imagine to be prejudicial either to religion or to the state, nor, as a consequence, had I found anything that would have prevented me from writing it, had reason persuaded me of it, and this made me fear that there might likewise be found among my opinions one in which I had been mistaken, notwithstanding the great care that I have always taken never to accept into my beliefs any new opinions for which I did not have very certain demonstrations and never to write anything that could turn to anyone's disadvantage. This was sufficient to make me change the resolution I had had to publish my opinions. For although the reasons for which I had earlier made the resolution were very strong, my inclination, which has always made me hate the business of writing books, immediately made me find enough other reasons to excuse me from it. And these reasons, both for and against, are such that not only do I have some interest in stating them here, but perhaps also the public has some interest in knowing them.

I had never made much of the things that came from my mind, and so long as I had reaped no other fruits from the method I am using except my own satisfaction regarding certain problems that pertain to the speculative sciences or else my attempt at governing my moral conduct by means of the reasons which the method taught me, I believed I was under no obligation whatever to write anything about it. For as to moral conduct, everyone is so very full of his own viewpoint, that it would be possible to find as many reformers as heads, if anyone other than those God has established as rulers over his peoples or even those to whom he has given sufficient grace and zeal to be prophets were permitted to try to change anything here. And although my speculations pleased me very much, I believed that others also had their own which perhaps pleased them more. But as soon as I had acquired some general notions regarding physics, and, beginning to test them in various particular difficulties, I had noticed where they could lead and how much they differ from the principles that have been in use up to the present, I believed I could not

---

10. Galileo Galilei (1564–1642), Italian astronomer, mathematician and physicist. His *Dialogue ... on the Two Chief Systems of the World* (1632), in which he advanced the theory of the movement of the earth, occasioned the Inquisitors of the Holy Office to conduct a trial in Rome and to extort a retraction of that theory from Galileo. Descartes, who also advocated a theory of terrestrial motion, was not about to let Rome sin twice against philosophy. Cf. E. Gilson, *Discours de la méthode: texte et commentaire*, pp. 439–42.

keep them hidden away without sinning grievously against the law that obliges us to procure, as much as is in our power, the common good of all men. For these notions made me see that it is possible to arrive at knowledge that would be very useful in life and that, in place of that speculative philosophy taught in the schools, it is possible to find a practical philosophy, by means of which, knowing the force and the actions of fire, water, air, the stars, the heavens, and all the other bodies that surround us, just as distinctly as we know the various skills of our craftsmen, we might be able, in the same way, to use them for all the purposes for which they are appropriate, and thus render ourselves, as it were, masters and possessors of nature. This is desirable not only for the invention of an infinity of devices that would enable one to enjoy trouble-free the fruits of the earth and all the goods found there, but also principally for the maintenance of health, which unquestionably is the first good and the foundation of all the other goods of this life, for even the mind depends so greatly on the temperament and on the disposition of the organs of the body that, if it is possible to find some means to render men generally more wise and more adroit than they have been up until now, I believe that one should look for it in medicine. It is true that the medicine currently practiced contains few things whose usefulness is so noteworthy, but without intending to ridicule it, I am sure there is no one, not even among those who make a profession of it, who would not admit that everything known in medicine is practically nothing in comparison with what remains to be known, and that one could rid oneself of an infinity of maladies, as much of the body as of the mind, and even perhaps also the frailty of old age, if one had a sufficient knowledge of their causes and of all the remedies that nature has provided us. For, having the intention of spending my entire life in the search for so indispensable a science, and having found a path that seems to me such that, by following it, one ought infallibly to find this science, unless one is prevented from doing so either by the brevity of life or by a lack of experiments,[11] I judged there to be no better remedy against these two obstacles than to communicate faithfully to the public the entirety of what little I had found and to urge good minds to try to advance beyond this by contributing, each according to his inclination and ability, to the experiments that must be performed and also by communicating to the public everything they might learn, in order that, with subsequent inquirers beginning where their predecessors had left off, and thus, joining together the lives and

---

11. *Expérience* is used by Descartes to refer to a wide range of activities, from simple observations to sophisticated scientific experiments. *Expérience* will be translated as "observations" or as "experiments," depending on the context.

labors of many, we might all advance together much further than a single individual could do on his own.

Moreover, I noticed, in regard to experiments, that they are the more necessary as one is more advanced in knowledge. For in the beginning it is better to make use only of those observations which present themselves of their own accord to our senses and which we could not ignore, provided we reflect, however so little, on them, rather than to search for unusual and contrived experiments. The reason for this is that these more unusual experiments often deceive one when one does not know yet the causes of the more common ones, and that the circumstances on which the unusual ones depend are almost always so special and so minute that it is very difficult to notice them. But the order I have held to has been the following.

64 First, I have tried to find in general the principles or first causes of all that is or can be in the world, without considering anything but God alone, who created the world, and without deriving these principles from any other source but from certain seeds of truths that are naturally in our souls. After that I examined what were the first and most ordinary effects that could be deduced from these causes; and it seems to me that by this means I had found the heavens, stars, an earth, and even, on the earth, water, air, fire, minerals, and other such things that are the most common of all and the simplest, and, as a consequence, the easiest to know. Then, when I wanted to descend to those things which were more particular, so many different ones were presented to me that I did not believe it possible for the human mind to distinguish the forms or species of bodies that are on the earth from an infinity of others that could have been there had it been the will of God to have put them there, nor, as a consequence, to make them serviceable to us, unless we advance to the causes through the effects and make use of many particular observations. After this, passing my mind again over all the objects that have ever presented themselves to my senses, I daresay I did not notice anything in them that I could not explain easily enough by means of the principles I had found. But I must also admit that the power of nature is so ample and so vast, and these principles are so simple and so general, that I notice hardly any
65 particular effect without at once knowing that it can be deduced in many different ways from them, and that ordinarily my greatest difficulty is to find in which of these ways it depends on them. For, to this end, I know of no other expedient at all except to search once more for some experiments which are such that their outcomes are not the same, if it is in one of these ways rather than in another that one ought to explain the outcome. As to the rest, I am now at the point where, it seems to me, I see quite well what approach one must take in order to make most of the experiments that can serve this purpose; but I also see that they are of

such a kind and of so great a number that neither my adroitness nor my financial resources (even if I had a thousand times more than I have) would suffice for all of them, so that, according as I henceforth have the opportunity to perform more or fewer experiments, I shall also advance more or less in the knowledge of nature. That is what I meant to make known through the treatise I had written, and to show there so clearly the utility that the public could gain from such knowledge that I would oblige all those who desire the general well-being of men (that is to say, all those who really are virtuous, not just appearing to be so through false pretenses or merely by reputation), both to communicate those experiments they have already performed and to assist me in the search for those that remain to be performed.

But since then other reasons have made me change my mind and to think that I really ought to continue to write about all the things I judged to be of some importance, to the extent that I discovered the truth with respect to them, and to take the same care in regard to them as I would take if I wanted to have them published. I did this as much to have all the more of an occasion to examine them well (since without doubt one always looks more carefully at what one believes must be seen by many than at what one does only for oneself, and often the things that have seemed to me to be true when I began to conceive them have appeared false to me when I wanted to put them on paper), as in order not to lose any occasion to benefit the public, if I am able, and in order that, if my writings are worth anything, those who will have them after my death can thus use them as will be most fitting. But I must not in any way consent to their being published during my lifetime, so that neither the hostilities and the controversies to which they might be subject, nor even such reputation as they could gain for me, would give me any occasion for losing the time I have intended to use in instructing myself. For although it may be true that each man is obliged to secure as best he can the good of others, and that to be useful to no one is, strictly speaking, to be worthless, still it is also true that our concerns ought to extend further than to the present time, and that it is well to omit things that perhaps would yield some profit to those who are alive, when it is with the intention of doing other things that would yield even more profit to our posterity. In any event, I very much want people to understand that what little I have learned up until now is almost nothing in comparison to what I do not know and to what I do not despair of being able to learn, for it is almost the same with those who little by little discover the truth in the sciences as it is with those who, upon beginning to acquire wealth, have less trouble making large acquisitions than they had had before, when they were poorer, in making very small ones. Or indeed, one can compare them to army commanders whose forces typically grow in proportion to their victories and who need more skill to maintain themselves after losing a battle than they do to take cities or provinces when they have won one. For it is truly to engage in battle when one tries to overcome all the difficulties and errors that prevent us from arriving at the knowledge of the truth, and it is truly to lose a battle when one accepts a false opinion touching on a matter that is at all general and important. And afterward it requires much more skill to recover one's former position than to make great progress when one already has principles that are assured. For myself, if I have already found some truths in the sciences (and I hope the things contained in this volume will make people judge that I have found some of them), I can say that these are only things that result from and depend on five or six principal difficulties that I have surmounted and that I count as so many battles in which I have had fortune on my side. I will not even fear to say that I think I need to win only two or three more battles like them in order to succeed entirely in my plans, and that my age is not at all so advanced that, in the ordinary course of nature, I might not still have enough time to bring this about. But I believe I am all the more obliged to manage well the time remaining to me, the more hope I have of being able to use it well, and doubtless I would have many opportunities to lose time, had I published the foundations of my physics. For although they are nearly all so evident that it is necessary only to understand them in order to believe them, and although there has not been a single one for which I did not believe I could give demonstrations, nevertheless, because it is impossible for them to be in agreement with all the diverse opinions of other men, I foresee that I would often be distracted by the disputes they would engender.

One could say that these disputes might be useful, as much in order that I be made aware of my faults, as in order that, if I had anything worthwhile to say, others would by this means have greater understanding of it, and that, since many can see more than one man alone, these others, by beginning right now to use it, might also help me with their discoveries. But, although I recognize that I am extremely prone to err and that I almost never rely on the first thoughts that come to me, still the experience I have of the objections that can be made against me prevents me from expecting any profit from them. For I have already often put to the test the judgments of those I took to be my friends, as well as of some others whom I took to be indifferent, and even of those too whose maliciousness and envy I knew would try hard enough to discover what affection would hide from my friends. But it has rarely happened that an objection has been raised against me that I had not at all foreseen, unless it was very far removed from my subject; thus I have almost never found any critic of my opinions who did not seem to me to be either less rigorous or less unbiased than myself. Nor have I ever observed that, through the method of disputations practiced in the schools, any truth has been discovered that had until then been unknown. For, so long as each person in the dispute aims at winning, he is more concerned with making much out of probability than with weighing the arguments on each side; and those who have long been good advocates are not, on that account, afterward better judges.

As to the utility that others might gain from the communication of my thoughts, it could not be so very great, given that I have not yet at all taken them so far that there is no need to add many things to them before applying them to actual practice. And I think I can say without vanity that, if there is anyone who is capable of doing this, it must be myself rather than someone else: not that there could not be in the world many minds incomparably greater than mine, but because one cannot conceive a thing so well and make it one's own when one learns it from someone else as one can when one discovers it for oneself. This is so true in this matter that, although I have often explained some of my opinions to people with good minds, who, while I spoke to them, seemed to understand them quite distinctly, nevertheless, when they repeated them, I noticed that they had almost always changed them in such a way that I could no longer acknowledge them as mine. In this connection, I am very happy here to ask our descendants never to believe the things people tell them came from me, unless I myself have divulged them. And I am in no way surprised by the extravagances attributed to all those ancient philosophers whose writings we do not have, nor do I judge, for that reason, that their thoughts have been so very unreasonable, given that they were the greatest minds of their time, but only that their thoughts have been poorly reported to us. For one also sees that it has almost never happened that any of their followers had ever surpassed them, and I am sure that the most impassioned of those who now follow Aristotle would believe themselves fortunate, if they had as much knowledge of nature as he had, even if it were on the condition that they would never have any more. They are like ivy, which never stretches any higher than the trees supporting it, and which often even descends again after it has reached their tops, for it seems to me that they too are redescending, that is, they are making themselves somehow less knowledgeable than if they abstained from studying; not content with knowing all that is intelligibly explained in their author, they want in addition to find the solutions there to many difficulties about which he says nothing and about which he has perhaps never thought. Still, their manner of philosophizing is very convenient for those who have only very mediocre minds, for the obscurity of the distinctions and the principles they make use of is the reason why they can speak about all things as boldly as if they knew them, and why they can uphold everything they say against the most subtle and the most adroit, without anyone's having the means of convincing them that they are mistaken. In this they seem to me like a blind man who, in order to fight without a disadvantage against someone who is sighted, had made his opponent go into the depths of some very dark cellar. And I may say that these people have an interest in my refraining from publishing the principles of the philosophy I use, for my principles being as very simple and very evident as they are, I would, by publishing them, be doing almost the same as if I were to open some windows and make some daylight enter that cellar they had gone into in order to fight. But even the best minds have no reason for wanting to know these principles, for if they want to know how to speak about all things and to acquire the reputation for being learned, they will achieve their objective more easily by contenting themselves with probability, which can be found without great difficulty in all sorts of matters, than by seeking the truth, which can only be discovered little by little in some and which, when it is a question of speaking about other matters, obliges one to confess frankly that one is ignorant of them. But if they prefer the knowledge of some few truths to the vanity of appearing to be ignorant of nothing, as no doubt it is really preferable to do, and if they want to follow a plan similar to mine, they do not, on that score, need me to say anything more except what I have already said in this discourse. For, if they are capable of advancing further than I have, then *a fortiori* they are also capable of finding for themselves all that I think I have found. Inasmuch as I have never examined anything except in an orderly manner, it is certain that what still remains for me to discover is of itself more difficult and more hidden than what I have heretofore been able to discover, and they would take much less pleasure in learning it from me than from themselves. Moreover, the habit they will acquire of seeking first the easy things and then of passing little by little by degrees to other more difficult ones will serve them better than all my instructions could do. As for myself, I am convinced that, if I had been taught from my youth all the truths for which I have since then sought demonstrations, and if I had not had any difficulty in learning them, I might perhaps have never known any other truths, and at least I would never have acquired the habit and facility I think I have for always finding new truths, to the extent that I apply myself in searching for them. And, in a word, if there is any task in the world that could not be accomplished so well by anyone else but the same person who began it, it is the one on which I am working.

It is true that, with respect to experiments that can help here, one man alone cannot suffice to perform them all, but neither can he usefully employ hands other than his own, except those of craftsmen, or such people as he could pay and whom the hope of gain, which is a very effective means, would cause to do precisely what he ordered them to do. For, as to volunteers, who, out of curiosity or a desire to learn, might offer themselves in order perhaps to help him (aside from the fact that they usually make more promises than they produce achievements, and merely make fine proposals, none of which will come to anything), they would inevitably want to be paid by the explanation of various difficulties, or at least by compliments and useless conversations, which could not cost him so little time that he would not lose by it. And as to the experiments that others have already performed, even if these people did want to communicate them to him (something those who call them "secrets" would never do), they are for the most part composed of so many details and superfluous ingredients that it would be very hard for him to discern the truth in them; besides, he would find almost all of them to be so badly explained or even so false, because those who have done them strove to make them appear to be in conformity with their principles, that, if there were among them some experiments that might serve him, they could not be worth the time he would need to spend in selecting them. In this way, if there were someone in the world whom one assuredly knows to be capable of finding the greatest things and the things as beneficial to the public as possible and whom, for this cause, other men were to exert themselves to help in every way to succeed in his plans, I do not see that they could do a thing for him except to make a donation toward the expenses of the experiments he would need and, for the rest, to prevent his leisure from being wasted by the importunity of anyone. But, although I do not presume so much of myself as to want to promise anything out of the ordinary, or feast on such vain thoughts as to imagine that the public ought to be especially interested in my plans, I do not have so base a soul that I would want to accept from anyone any favor that one might believe I had not deserved.

All these considerations taken together were the reason why, three years ago, I did not at all want to divulge the treatise I had on hand, and why I had even made a resolution not to make public during my lifetime any other treatise which was so general or on the basis of which one could understand the foundations of my physics. But since then there have been yet again two other reasons that have obliged me to place here certain particular essays and to render to the public some account of my actions and my plans. The first is that, if I failed to do so, many who knew of the intention I once had to have certain writings published could imagine that the reasons for which I am abstaining from doing so were more to my disadvantage than they are. For although I do not love glory excessively—

indeed, if I dare say so, I hate it, inasmuch as I judge it to be contrary to the tranquility I esteem above all things—still, I have also never tried to hide my actions as if they were crimes, nor have I taken many precautions so as not to be known. This is the case as much because I would have believed I would be doing myself an injustice, as because it would have given me a certain kind of disquiet, which again would have been contrary to the perfect peace of mind I am seeking. And because, having always been thus indifferent about the concern over being known or not known, I could not prevent my acquiring some type of reputation, I thought I ought to do my best at least to spare myself from having a bad one. The other reason that has obliged me to write this is as follows: I saw more and more every day the delay that the plan I have of self-instruction is suffering because of an infinity of experiments of which I have need and which it is impossible for me to perform without the help of others. And although I do not flatter myself so much as to hope that the public will become greatly taken with my interests, still I also do not want to fail myself so much as to give those who will survive me cause to reproach me one day on the grounds that I could have left them many far better things than I had done, if I had not so badly neglected making them understand how they could contribute to my plans.

And I thought that it was easy to choose certain matters that, without being subjected to much controversy or obliging me to declare more of my principles than I desire, would nevertheless allow me to show quite clearly what I can or cannot do in the sciences. I cannot say whether I have been successful in this, and I do not at all want to prejudice the judgments of anyone in speaking for myself about my writings; but I shall be very happy if they are examined, and, in order to have more of an opportunity to do this, I am imploring all who have any objections to make against them to take the trouble to send them to my publisher and, on being advised about them by him, I shall try at the same time to append my reply to the objections, and by this means, seeing both of them together, readers will judge the truth all the more easily. For I promise never to make long replies to them, but only to admit my errors very candidly, if I recognize them, or, even if I cannot perceive any, to say simply what I believe to be required for the defense of what I have written, without adding to it an explanation of any new material, in order not to become endlessly involved in one issue after another.

And, if any of those things about which I have spoken at the beginning of the *Dioptrics* and the *Meteors* are shocking at first glance because I call them suppositions and seem to lack the inclination to prove them, I entreat the reader to have the patience to read the whole thing with attention, and I hope he will find himself satisfied with it. For it seems to me that the reasonings follow each other there in such a way that, just as the last are demonstrated by means of the first, which are their causes, so these first are reciprocally demonstrated by means of the last, which are their effects. And one must not imagine that I am here committing the fallacy that logicians call a circle, for, experience rendering the majority of these effects very certain, the causes from which I deduce these effects serve not so much to prove them as to explain them; on the contrary, it is rather the case that the causes are what are proved by the effects. And I have called them suppositions only to make it understood that I think I can deduce them from these first truths that I have explained above. But I wanted expressly not to do so, in order to prevent certain minds, who imagine that they know in one day all that someone else has thought about for twenty years as soon as he has said but two or three words to them about it, and who are the more subject to error and the less capable of truth, the more penetrating and lively they are, from being able to take this occasion to build some extravagant philosophy on what they believe are my principles, and in order to prevent me from being blamed for it. For as to the opinions that are entirely mine, I do not apologize for their being new, since, if one considers well the arguments for them, I am sure that one will find them so simple and so in conformity with common sense that they will seem less extraordinary and less strange than any others one could have on the same subjects. Nor do I pride myself at all on being the first discoverer of any of them; rather, I pride myself on never having accepted them because they have or have not been said by others, but only because reason has persuaded me of them.

If craftsmen cannot immediately carry out the invention explained in the *Dioptrics,* I do not believe one could say, on that account, that it is bad, for, inasmuch as skill and practice are needed to make and adjust the machines I have described, without any detail being overlooked there, I would be no less astonished if they were to succeed on the first try than if someone were able to learn in one day to play the lute with distinction simply because he had been given a good score. And if I write in French, the language of my country, rather than in Latin, the language of my teachers, it is because I am hoping that those who use only their natural reason in all its purity will judge my opinions better than those who believe only in old books. And as to those who combine good sense with study, whom alone I wish to have as my judges, they will not at all, I am sure, be so partial to Latin that they refuse to listen to my reasons because I explain them in the vernacular.

As to the rest, I do not at all want to speak here in detail about the future progress I hope to make in the sciences, or to involve myself vis-à-vis the public in any promise that I am not assured of keeping; rather

I shall say simply that I have resolved to spend the rest of my life on nothing but trying to acquire some knowledge of nature which is such that one could draw from it rules for medicine that are more reliable than those we have had to the present, and that my inclination puts me at such a great distance from all other sorts of plans, and chiefly from those that can be useful to some only by being harmful to others, that if circumstances were to force me to busy myself with them, I do not at all believe I could succeed. About this I am here making a declaration which I know very well cannot serve to make me eminent in the world, but I also have no desire to be so; and I shall always hold myself obliged more to those by whose favor I enjoy my leisure without hindrance than to those who might offer me the most honorable positions on earth.

END

Meditations
on
First Philosophy

NOTE ON THE TRANSLATION

The translation is based entirely on the Latin version of the *Meditations* found in volume seven of the Adam and Tannery edition of Descartes' works. It has been argued by Baillet, Descartes's early biographer, that the French "translation" by de Luynes is superior to the Latin version because it contains many additions and clarifications made by Descartes himself. However, I have not used the French version, because it contains inconsistencies and shifts that muddle more than clarify the original Latin text. The numbers found in the margins of the present translation refer to the page numbers of the Latin text in the Adam and Tannery edition.

In one instance, I found that the Latin text did not square with Descartes' clear intention. A footnote conveys my suggestion as to Descartes's actual intention in the passage.

D.A.C.

*To those Most Wise and Distinguished Men,
the Dean and Doctors of the Faculty of Sacred Theology of Paris*
René Descartes Sends Greetings

So right is the cause that impels me to offer this work to you, that I am confident you too will find it equally right and thus take up its defense, once you have understood the plan of my undertaking; so much is this the case that I have no better means of commending it here than to state briefly what I have sought to achieve in this work.

I have always thought that two issues—namely, God and the soul—are chief among those that ought to be demonstrated with the aid of philosophy rather than theology. For although it suffices for us believers to believe by faith that the human soul does not die with the body, and that God exists, certainly no unbelievers seem capable of being persuaded of any religion or even of almost any moral virtue, until these two are first proven to them by natural reason. And since in this life greater rewards are often granted to vices than to virtues, few would prefer what is right to what is useful, if they neither feared God nor anticipated an afterlife. Granted, it is altogether true that we must believe in God's existence because it is taught in the Holy Scriptures, and, conversely, that we must believe the Holy Scriptures because they have come from God. This is because, of course, since faith is a gift from God, the very same one who gives the grace that is necessary for believing the rest can also give the grace to believe that he exists. Nonetheless, this reasoning cannot be proposed to unbelievers because they would judge it to be circular. In fact, I have observed that not only do you and all other theologians affirm that one can prove the existence of God by natural reason, but also that one may infer from Sacred Scripture that the knowledge of him is easier to achieve than the many things we know about creatures, and is so utterly easy that those without this knowledge are blameworthy. For this is clear from *Wisdom*, Chapter 13, where it is said: "They are not to be excused, for if their capacity for knowing were so great that they could think well of this world, how is it that they did not find the Lord of it even more easily?" And in *Romans*, Chapter 1, it is said that they are "without excuse." And again in the same passage it appears we are being warned with the words: "What is known of God is manifest in them," that everything that can be known about God can be shown by reasons drawn exclusively from our own mind. For this reason, I did not think it unbecoming for me to inquire how this may be the case, and by what path God may be known more easily and with greater certainty than the things of this world.

3   And as to the soul, there are many who have regarded its nature as something into which one cannot easily inquire, and some have even gone so far as to say that human reasoning convinces them that the soul dies with the body, while it is by faith alone that they hold the contrary position. Nevertheless, because the Lateran Council held under Leo X, in Session 8, condemned such people and expressly enjoined Christian philosophers to refute their arguments and to use all their powers to demonstrate the truth, I have not hesitated to undertake this task as well.

Moreover, I know that there are many irreligious people who refuse to believe that God exists and that the human mind is distinct from the body—for no other reason than their claim that up until now no one has been able to demonstrate these two things. By no means am I in agreement with these people; on the contrary, I believe that nearly all the arguments which have been brought to bear on these questions by great men have the force of a demonstration, when they are adequately understood, and I am convinced that hardly any arguments can be given that have not already been discovered by others. Nevertheless, I judge that there is no greater task to perform in philosophy than assiduously to seek out, once and for all, the best of all these arguments and to lay them out so precisely and plainly that henceforth all will take them to be true demonstrations. And finally, I was strongly urged to do this by some people who knew that I had developed a method for solving all sorts of problems in the sciences—not a new one, mind you, since nothing is more ancient than the truth, but one they had seen me use with some success in other areas. Accordingly, I took it to be my task to attempt something on this subject.

4   This treatise contains all that I have been able to accomplish. Not that I have attempted to gather together in it all the various arguments that could be brought forward as proof of the very same conclusions, for this does not seem worthwhile, except where no one proof is sufficiently certain. Rather, I have sought out the primary and chief arguments, so that I now make bold to propose these as most certain and evident demonstrations. Moreover, I will say in addition that these arguments are such that I believe there is no way open to the human mind whereby better ones could ever be found. For the urgency of the cause, as well as the glory of God, to which this entire enterprise is referred, compels me here to speak somewhat more freely on my own behalf than is my custom. But although I believe these arguments to be certain and evident, still I am not thereby convinced that they are suited to everyone's grasp. In geometry there are many arguments developed by Archimedes, Apollonius, Pappus, and others, which are taken by everyone to be evident and certain because they contain absolutely nothing which, considered by itself, is not quite easily known, and in which what follows does not square

exactly with what has come before. Nevertheless they are rather lengthy and require a particularly attentive reader; thus only a small handful of people understand them. Likewise, although the arguments I use here do, in my opinion, equal or even surpass those of geometry in certitude and obviousness, nevertheless I am fearful that many people will not be capable of adequately perceiving them, both because they too are a bit lengthy, with some of them depending on still others, and also because, first and foremost, they demand a mind that is quite free from prejudices and that can easily withdraw itself from association with the senses. Certainly there are not to be found in the world more people with an aptitude for metaphysical studies than those with an aptitude for geometry. Moreover, there is the difference that in geometry everyone is of a mind that usually nothing is put down in writing without there being a sound demonstration for it; thus the inexperienced more frequently err on the side of assenting to what is false, wanting as they do to give the appearance of understanding it, than on the side of denying what is true. But it is the reverse in philosophy: since it is believed that there is no issue that cannot be defended from either side, few look for the truth, and many more prowl about for a reputation for profundity by arrogantly challenging whichever arguments are the best.

And therefore, regardless of the force of my arguments, because they are of a philosophical nature I do not anticipate that what I will have accomplished through them will be very worthwhile unless you assist me with your patronage. Your faculty is held in such high esteem in the minds of all, and the name of the Sorbonne has such authority, that not only in matters of faith has no association, with the exception of the councils of the Church, been held in such high regard as yours, but even in human philosophy nowhere is there thought to be greater insightfulness and solidity, or greater integrity and wisdom in rendering judgments. Should you deign to show any interest in this work, I do not doubt that, first of all, its errors would be corrected by you (for I am mindful not only of my humanity but also, and most especially, of my ignorance, and thus do not claim that there are no errors in it); second, what is lacking would be added, or what is not sufficiently complete would be perfected, or what is in need of further discussion would be expanded upon more fully, either by yourselves or at least by me, after you have given me your guidance; and finally, after the arguments contained in this work proving that God exists and that the mind is distinct from the body have been brought (as I am confident they can be) to such a level of lucidity that these arguments ought to be regarded as the most precise of demonstrations, you may be of a mind to make such a declaration and publicly attest to it. Indeed, should this come to pass, I have no doubt that all the errors that have ever been entertained regarding these issues would shortly be erased from the minds of men. For the truth itself will easily cause other men of intelligence and learning to subscribe to your judgment. Your authority will cause the atheists, who more often than not are dilettantes rather than men of intelligence and learning, to put aside their spirit of contrariness, and perhaps even to defend the arguments which they will come to know are regarded as demonstrations by all who are discerning, lest they appear not to understand them. And finally, everyone else will readily give credence to so many indications of support, and there will no longer be anyone in the world who would dare call into doubt either the existence of God or the real distinction between the soul and the body. Just how great the usefulness of this thing might be, you yourselves, in virtue of your singular wisdom, are in the best position of anyone to judge; nor would it behoove me to commend the cause of God and religion at any greater length to you, who have always been the greatest pillar of the Catholic Church.

Preface to the Reader

I have already touched briefly on the issues of God and the human mind in my *Discourse on the Method of Rightly Conducting One's Reason and Searching for Truth in the Sciences*, published in French in 1637. The intent there was not to provide a precise treatment of them, but only to offer a sample and to learn from the opinions of readers how these issues should be treated in the future. For they seemed to me to be so important that I judged they ought to be dealt with more than once. And the path I follow in order to explain them is so little trodden and so far removed from the one commonly taken that I did not think it useful to hold forth at greater length in a work written in French and designed to be read indiscriminately by everyone, lest weaker minds be in a position to think that they too ought to set out on this path.

In the *Discourse* I asked everyone who might find something in my writings worthy of refutation to do me the favor of making me aware of it. As for what I touched on regarding these issues, only two objections were worth noting, and I will respond briefly to them here before undertaking a more precise explanation of them.

The first is that, from the fact that the human mind, when turned in on itself, does not perceive itself to be anything other than a thinking thing, it does not follow that its nature or *essence* consists only in its being a thinking thing, such that the word *only* excludes everything else that also could perhaps be said to belong to the nature of the soul. To this objection I answer that in that passage I did not intend my exclusion of those things to reflect the order of the truth of the matter (I was not dealing with it then), but merely the order of my perception. Thus what I had in mind was that I was aware of absolutely nothing that I knew belonged to my essence, save that I was a thinking thing, that is, a thing having within itself the faculty of thinking. Later on, however, I will show how it follows, from the fact that I know of nothing else belonging to my essence, that nothing else really does belong to it.

The second objection is that it does not follow from the fact that I have within me an idea of a thing more perfect than me, that this idea is itself more perfect than me, and still less that what is represented by this idea exists. But I answer that there is an equivocation here in the word "idea." For "idea" can be taken either materially, for an operation of the intellect (in which case it cannot be said to be more perfect than me), or objectively, for the thing represented by means of that operation. This thing, even if it is not presumed to exist outside the intellect, can nevertheless be more perfect than me by reason of its essence. I will explain in detail in the ensuing remarks how, from the mere fact that there is within me an idea of something more perfect than me, it follows that this thing really exists.

In addition, I have seen two rather lengthy treatises, but these works, utilizing as they do arguments drawn from atheist commonplaces, focused their attack not so much on my arguments regarding these issues, as on my conclusions. Moreover, arguments of this type exercise no influence over those who understand my arguments, and the judgments of many people are so preposterous and feeble that they are more likely to be persuaded by the first opinions to come along, however false and contrary to reason they may be, than by a true and firm refutation of them which they hear subsequently. Accordingly, I have no desire to respond here to these objections, lest I first have to state what they are. I will only say in general that all the objections typically bandied about by the atheists to assail the existence of God always depend either on ascribing human emotions to God, or on arrogantly claiming for our minds such power and wisdom that we attempt to determine and grasp fully what God can and ought to do. Hence these objections will cause us no difficulty, provided we but remember that our minds are to be regarded as finite, while God is to be regarded as incomprehensible and infinite.

But now, after having, to some degree, conducted an initial review of the judgments of men, here I begin once more to treat the same questions about God and the human mind, together with the starting points of the whole of first philosophy, but not in a way that causes me to have any expectation of widespread approval or a large readership. On the contrary, I do not advise anyone to read these things except those who have both the ability and the desire to meditate seriously with me, and to withdraw their minds from the senses as well as from all prejudices. I know all too well that such people are few and far between. As to those who do not take the time to grasp the order and linkage of my arguments, but will be eager to fuss over statements taken out of context (as is the custom for many), they will derive little benefit from reading this work. Although perhaps they might find an occasion for quibbling in several places, still they will not find it easy to raise an objection that is either compelling or worthy of response.

But because I do not promise to satisfy even the others on all counts the first time around, and because I do not arrogantly claim for myself so much that I believe myself capable of anticipating all the difficulties that will occur to someone, I will first of all narrate in the *Meditations* the very thoughts by means of which I seem to have arrived at a certain and evident knowledge of the truth, so that I may determine whether the same arguments that persuaded me can be useful in persuading others. Next, I will reply to the objections of a number of very gifted and learned gentlemen, to whom these *Meditations* were forwarded for their examination prior to their being sent to press. For their objections were so many and varied that I have dared to hope that nothing will readily occur to anyone, at least nothing of importance, which has not already been touched upon by these gentlemen. And thus I earnestly entreat the readers not to form a judgment regarding the *Meditations* until they have deigned to read all these objections and the replies I have made to them.

Synopsis of the Following Six Meditations

In the First Meditation the reasons are given why we can doubt all things, especially material things, so long, that is, as, of course, we have no other foundations for the sciences than the ones which we have had up until now. Although the utility of so extensive a doubt is not readily apparent, nevertheless its greatest utility lies in freeing us of all prejudices, in preparing the easiest way for us to withdraw the mind from the senses, and finally, in making it impossible for to us doubt any further those things that we later discover to be true.

In the Second Meditation the mind, through the exercise of its own freedom, supposes the nonexistence of all those things about whose existence it can have even the least doubt. In so doing the mind realizes that it is impossible for it not to exist during this time. This too is of the greatest utility, since by means of it the mind easily distinguishes what things belong to it, that is, to an intellectual nature, from what things belong to the body. But because some people will perhaps expect to see proofs for the immortality of the soul in this Meditation, I think they should be put on notice here that I have attempted to write only what I have carefully demonstrated. Therefore the only order I could follow was the one typically used by geometers, which is to lay out everything on which a given proposition depends, before concluding anything about it. But the first and principal prerequisite for knowing that the soul is immortal is that we form a concept of the soul that is as lucid as possible and utterly distinct from every concept of a body. This is what has been done here. Moreover, there is the additional requirement that we know that everything that we clearly and distinctly understand is true, in exactly the manner in which we understand it; however, this could not have been proven prior to the Fourth Meditation. Moreover, we must have a distinct concept of corporeal nature, and this is formulated partly in the Second Meditation itself, and partly in the Fifth and Sixth Meditations. From all this one ought to conclude that all the things we clearly and distinctly conceive as different substances truly are substances that are really distinct from one another. (This, for example, is how mind and body are conceived.) This conclusion is arrived at in the Sixth Meditation. This same conclusion is also confirmed in this Meditation in virtue of the fact that we cannot understand a body to be anything but divisible, whereas we cannot understand the mind to be anything but indivisible. For we cannot conceive of half of a mind, as we can half of any body whatever, no matter how small. From this we are prompted to acknowledge that the natures of mind and body not only are different from one another, but even, in a manner of speaking, are contraries of one another. However, I have not written any further on the matter in this work, both because these considerations suffice for showing that the annihilation of the mind does not follow from the decaying of the body (and thus these considerations suffice for giving mortals hope in an afterlife), and also because the premises from which the immortality of the mind can be inferred depend upon an account of the whole of physics. First, we need to know that absolutely all substances, that is, things that must be created by God in order to exist, are by their very nature incorruptible, and can never cease to exist, unless, by the same God's denying his concurrence to them, they be reduced to nothingness. Second, we need to realize that body, taken in a general sense, is a substance and hence it too can never perish. But the human body, insofar as it differs from other bodies, is composed of merely a certain configuration of members, together with other accidents of the same sort. But the human mind is not likewise composed of any accidents, but is a pure substance. For even if all its accidents were changed, so that it understands different things, wills different things, senses different things, and so on, the mind itself does not on that score become something different. On the other hand, the human body does become something different, merely as a result of the fact that a change in the shape of some of its parts has taken place. It follows from these considerations that a body can very easily perish, whereas the mind by its nature is immortal.

In the Third Meditation I have explained at sufficient length, it seems to me, my principal argument for proving the existence of God. Nevertheless, since my intent was to draw the minds of readers as far as possible from the senses, I had no desire to draw upon comparisons based upon corporeal things. Thus many obscurities may perhaps have remained; but these, I trust, will later be entirely removed in my Replies to the Objections. One such point of contention, among others, is the following: how can the idea that is in us of a supremely perfect being have so much objective reality that it can only come from a supremely perfect cause? This is illustrated in the Replies by a comparison with a very perfect machine, the idea of which is in the mind of some craftsman. For, just as the objective ingeniousness of this idea ought to have some cause (say, the knowledge possessed by the craftsman or by someone else from whom he received this knowledge), so too, the idea of God which is in us must have God himself as its cause.

In the Fourth Meditation it is proved that all that we clearly and distinctly perceive is true, and it is also explained what constitutes the nature of falsity. These things necessarily need to be known both to confirm what has preceded as well as to help readers understand what remains. (But here one should meanwhile bear in mind that in that

Meditation there is no discussion whatsoever of sin, that is, the error committed in the pursuit of good and evil, but only the error that occurs in discriminating between what is true and what is false. Nor is there an examination of those matters pertaining to the faith or to the conduct of life, but merely of speculative truths known exclusively by means of the light of nature.)

In the Fifth Meditation, in addition to an explanation of corporeal nature in general, the existence of God is also demonstrated by means of a new proof. But again several difficulties may arise here; however, these are resolved later in my Replies to the Objections. Finally, it is shown how it is true that the certainty of even geometrical demonstrations depends upon the knowledge of God.

Finally, in the Sixth Meditation the understanding is distinguished from the imagination and the marks of this distinction are described. The mind is proved to be really distinct from the body, even though the mind is shown to be so closely joined to the body that it forms a single unit with it. All the errors commonly arising from the senses are reviewed; an account of the ways in which these errors can be avoided is provided. Finally, all the arguments on the basis of which we may infer the existence of material things are presented—not because I believed them to be very useful for proving what they prove, namely, that there really is a world, that men have bodies, and the like (things which no one of sound mind has ever seriously doubted), but rather because, through a consideration of these arguments, one realizes that they are neither so firm nor so evident as the arguments leading us to the knowledge of our mind and of God, so that, of all the things that can be known by the human mind, these latter are the most certain and the most evident. Proving this one thing was for me the goal of these Meditations. For this reason I will not review here the various issues that are also to be treated in these Meditations as the situation arises.

Meditations on First Philosophy

In Which the Existence of God and the Distinction between the Soul and the Body Are Demonstrated

MEDITATIONS ON FIRST PHILOSOPHY IN WHICH THE EXISTENCE OF GOD AND THE DISTINCTION BETWEEN THE SOUL AND THE BODY ARE DEMONSTRATED

Meditation One: Concerning Those Things That Can Be Called into Doubt

Several years have now passed since I first realized how numerous were the false opinions that in my youth I had taken to be true, and thus how doubtful were all those that I had subsequently built upon them. And thus I realized that once in my life I had to raze everything to the ground and begin again from the original foundations, if I wanted to establish anything firm and lasting in the sciences. But the task seemed enormous, and I was waiting until I reached a point in my life that was so timely that no more suitable time for undertaking these plans of action would come to pass. For this reason, I procrastinated for so long that I would henceforth be at fault, were I to waste the time that remains for carrying out the project by brooding over it. Accordingly, I have today suitably freed my mind of all cares, secured for myself a period of leisurely tranquillity, and am withdrawing into solitude. At last I will apply myself earnestly and unreservedly to this general demolition of my opinions.

Yet to bring this about I will not need to show that all my opinions are false, which is perhaps something I could never accomplish. But reason now persuades me that I should withhold my assent no less carefully from opinions that are not completely certain and indubitable than I would from those that are patently false. For this reason, it will suffice for the rejection of all of these opinions, if I find in each of them some reason for doubt. Nor therefore need I survey each opinion individually, a task that would be endless. Rather, because undermining the foundations will cause whatever has been built upon them to crumble of its own accord, I will attack straightaway those principles which supported everything I once believed.

Surely whatever I had admitted until now as most true I received either from the senses or through the senses. However, I have noticed that the senses are sometimes deceptive; and it is a mark of prudence never to place our complete trust in those who have deceived us even once.

But perhaps, even though the senses do sometimes deceive us when it is a question of very small and distant things, still there are many other matters concerning which one simply cannot doubt, even though they are derived from the very same senses: for example, that I am sitting here next to the fire, wearing my winter dressing gown, that I am holding this sheet of paper in my hands, and the like. But on what grounds could one deny that these hands and this entire body are mine? Unless perhaps I were to liken myself to the insane, whose brains are impaired by such an unrelenting vapor of black bile that they steadfastly insist that they are kings when they are utter paupers, or that they are arrayed in purple robes when they are naked, or that they have heads made of clay, or that they are gourds, or that they are made of glass. But such people are mad, and I would appear no less mad, were I to take their behavior as an example for myself.

This would all be well and good, were I not a man who is accustomed to sleeping at night, and to experiencing in my dreams the very same things, or now and then even less plausible ones, as these insane people do when they are awake. How often does my evening slumber persuade me of such ordinary things as these: that I am here, clothed in my dressing gown, seated next to the fireplace—when in fact I am lying undressed in bed! But right now my eyes are certainly wide awake when I gaze upon this sheet of paper. This head which I am shaking is not heavy with sleep. I extend this hand consciously and deliberately, and I feel it. Such things would not be so distinct for someone who is asleep. As if I did not recall having been deceived on other occasions even by similar thoughts in my dreams! As I consider these matters more carefully, I see so plainly that there are no definitive signs by which to distinguish being awake from being asleep. As a result, I am becoming quite dizzy, and this dizziness nearly convinces me that I am asleep.

Let us assume then, for the sake of argument, that we are dreaming and that such particulars as these are not true: that we are opening our eyes, moving our head, and extending our hands. Perhaps we do not even have such hands, or any such body at all. Nevertheless, it surely must be admitted that the things seen during slumber are, as it were, like painted images, which could only have been produced in the likeness of true things, and that therefore at least these general things—eyes, head, hands, and the whole body—are not imaginary things, but are true and exist. For indeed when painters themselves wish to represent sirens and satyrs by means of especially bizarre forms, they surely cannot assign to them utterly new natures. Rather, they simply fuse together the members of various animals. Or if perhaps they concoct something so utterly novel that nothing like it has ever been seen before (and thus is something utterly fictitious and false), yet certainly at the very least the colors from which they fashion it ought to be true. And by the same token, although even these general things—eyes, head, hands and the like—could be imaginary, still one has to admit that at least certain other things that are even more simple and universal are true. It is from these components, as if from true colors, that all those images of things that are in our thought are fashioned, be they true or false.

This class of things appears to include corporeal nature in general, together with its extension; the shape of extended things; their quantity, that is, their size and number; as well as the place where they exist; the time through which they endure, and the like.

Thus it is not improper to conclude from this that physics, astronomy, medicine, and all the other disciplines that are dependent upon the consideration of composite things are doubtful, and that, on the other hand, arithmetic, geometry, and other such disciplines, which treat of nothing but the simplest and most general things and which are indifferent as to whether these things do or do not in fact exist, contain something certain and indubitable. For whether I am awake or asleep, two plus three make five, and a square does not have more than four sides. It does not seem possible that such obvious truths should be subject to the suspicion of being false.

Be that as it may, there is fixed in my mind a certain opinion of long standing, namely that there exists a God who is able to do anything and by whom I, such as I am, have been created. How do I know that he did not bring it about that there is no earth at all, no heavens, no extended thing, no shape, no size, no place, and yet bringing it about that all these things appear to me to exist precisely as they do now? Moreover, since I judge that others sometimes make mistakes in matters that they believe they know most perfectly, may I not, in like fashion, be deceived every time I add two and three or count the sides of a square, or perform an even simpler operation, if that can be imagined? But perhaps God has not willed that I be deceived in this way, for he is said to be supremely good. Nonetheless, if it were repugnant to his goodness to have created me such that I be deceived all the time, it would also seem foreign to that same goodness to permit me to be deceived even occasionally. But we cannot make this last assertion.

Perhaps there are some who would rather deny so powerful a God than believe that everything else is uncertain. Let us not oppose them; rather, let us grant that everything said here about God is fictitious. Now they suppose that I came to be what I am either by fate, or by chance, or by a connected chain of events, or by some other way. But because being deceived and being mistaken appear to be a certain imperfection, the less powerful they take the author of my origin to be, the more probable it will be that I am so imperfect that I am always deceived. I have nothing to say in response to these arguments. But eventually I am forced to admit that there is nothing among the things I once believed to be true which it is not permissible to doubt—and not out of frivolity or lack of forethought, but for valid and considered reasons. Thus I must be no less careful to withhold assent henceforth even from these beliefs than I would from those that are patently false, if I wish to find anything certain.

But it is not enough simply to have realized these things; I must take steps to keep myself mindful of them. For long-standing opinions keep returning, and, almost against my will, they take advantage of my credulity, as if it were bound over to them by long use and the claims of intimacy. Nor will I ever get out of the habit of assenting to them and believing in them, so long as I take them to be exactly what they are, namely, in some respects doubtful, as has just now been shown, but nevertheless highly probable, so that it is much more consonant with reason to believe them than to deny them. Hence, it seems to me I would do well to deceive myself by turning my will in completely the opposite direction and pretend for a time that these opinions are wholly false and imaginary, until finally, as if with prejudices weighing down each side equally, no bad habit should turn my judgment any further from the correct perception of things. For indeed I know that meanwhile there is no danger or error in following this procedure, and that it is impossible for me to indulge in too much distrust, since I am now concentrating only on knowledge, not on action.

Accordingly, I will suppose not a supremely good God, the source of truth, but rather an evil genius, supremely powerful and clever, who has directed his entire effort at deceiving me. I will regard the heavens, the air, the earth, colors, shapes, sounds, and all external things as nothing but the bedeviling hoaxes of my dreams, with which he lays snares for my credulity. I will regard myself as not having hands, or eyes, or flesh, or blood, or any senses, but as nevertheless falsely believing that I possess all these things. I will remain resolute and steadfast in this meditation, and even if it is not within my power to know anything true, it certainly is within my power to take care resolutely to withhold my assent to what is false, lest this deceiver, however powerful, however clever he may be, have any effect on me. But this undertaking is arduous, and a certain laziness brings me back to my customary way of living. I am not unlike a prisoner who enjoyed an imaginary freedom during his sleep, but, when he later begins to suspect that he is dreaming, fears being awakened and nonchalantly conspires with these pleasant illusions. In just the same way, I fall back of my own accord into my old opinions, and dread being awakened, lest the toilsome wakefulness which follows upon a peaceful rest must be spent thenceforward not in the light but among the inextricable shadows of the difficulties now brought forward.

MEDITATION TWO: Concerning the Nature of the Human Mind: That It Is Better Known Than the Body

Yesterday's meditation has thrown me into such doubts that I can no longer ignore them, yet I fail to see how they are to be resolved. It is as if I had suddenly fallen into a deep whirlpool; I am so tossed about that I can neither touch bottom with my foot, nor swim up to the top. Nevertheless I will work my way up and will once again attempt the same path I entered upon yesterday. I will accomplish this by putting aside everything that admits of the least doubt, as if I had discovered it to be completely false. I will stay on this course until I know something certain, or, if nothing else, until I at least know for certain that nothing is certain. Archimedes sought but one firm and immovable point in order to move the entire earth from one place to another. Just so, great things are also to be hoped for if I succeed in finding just one thing, however slight, that is certain and unshaken.

Therefore I suppose that everything I see is false. I believe that none of what my deceitful memory represents ever existed. I have no senses whatever. Body, shape, extension, movement, and place are all chimeras. What then will be true? Perhaps just the single fact that nothing is certain.

But how do I know there is not something else, over and above all those things that I have just reviewed, concerning which there is not even the slightest occasion for doubt? Is there not some God, or by whatever name I might call him, who instills these very thoughts in me? But why would I think that, since I myself could perhaps be the author of these thoughts? Am I not then at least something? But I have already denied that I have any senses and any body. Still I hesitate; for what follows from this? Am I so tied to a body and to the senses that I cannot exist without them? But I have persuaded myself that there is absolutely nothing in the world: no sky, no earth, no minds, no bodies. Is it then the case that I too do not exist? But doubtless I did exist, if I persuaded myself of something. But there is some deceiver or other who is supremely powerful and supremely sly and who is always deliberately deceiving me. Then too there is no doubt that I exist, if he is deceiving me. And let him do his best at deception, he will never bring it about that I am nothing so long as I shall think that I am something. Thus, after everything has been most carefully weighed, it must finally be established that this pronouncement "I am, I exist" is necessarily true every time I utter it or conceive it in my mind.

But I do not yet understand sufficiently what I am—I, who now necessarily exist. And so from this point on, I must be careful lest I unwittingly mistake something else for myself, and thus err in that very item of knowledge that I claim to be the most certain and evident of all. Thus, I will meditate once more on what I once believed myself to be, prior to embarking upon these thoughts. For this reason, then, I will set aside whatever can be weakened even to the slightest degree by the arguments brought forward, so that eventually all that remains is precisely nothing but what is certain and unshaken.

What then did I use to think I was? A man, of course. But what is a man? Might I not say a "rational animal"? No, because then I would have to inquire what "animal" and "rational" mean. And thus from one question I would slide into many more difficult ones. Nor do I now have enough free time that I want to waste it on subtleties of this sort. Instead, permit me to focus here on what came spontaneously and naturally into my thinking whenever I pondered what I was. Now it occurred to me first that I had a face, hands, arms, and this entire mechanism of bodily members: the very same as are discerned in a corpse, and which I referred to by the name "body." It next occurred to me that I took in food, that I walked about, and that I sensed and thought various things; these actions I used to attribute to the soul. But as to what this soul might be, I either did not think about it or else I imagined it a rarified I-know-not-what, like a wind, or a fire, or ether, which had been infused into my coarser parts. But as to the body I was not in any doubt. On the contrary, I was under the impression that I knew its nature distinctly. Were I perhaps tempted to describe this nature such as I conceived it in my mind, I would have described it thus: by "body," I understand all that is capable of being bounded by some shape, of being enclosed in a place, and of filling up a space in such a way as to exclude any other body from it; of being perceived by touch, sight, hearing, taste, or smell; of being moved in several ways, not, of course, by itself, but by whatever else impinges upon it. For it was my view that the power of self-motion, and likewise of sensing or of thinking, in no way belonged to the nature of the body. Indeed I used rather to marvel that such faculties were to be found in certain bodies.

But now what am I, when I suppose that there is some supremely powerful and, if I may be permitted to say so, malicious deceiver who deliberately tries to fool me in any way he can? Can I not affirm that I possess at least a small measure of all those things which I have already said belong to the nature of the body? I focus my attention on them, I think about them, I review them again, but nothing comes to mind. I am tired of repeating this to no purpose. But what about those things I ascribed to the soul? What about being nourished or moving about? Since I now do not have a body, these are surely nothing but fictions. What about sensing? Surely this too does not take place without a body; and I seemed to have sensed in my dreams many things that I later realized I did not sense. What about thinking? Here I make my discovery: thought exists; it alone cannot be separated from me. I am; I exist—this is certain. But for how long? For as long as I am thinking; for perhaps it could also come to pass that if I were to cease all thinking I would then utterly cease to exist. At this time I admit nothing that is not necessarily true. I am therefore precisely nothing but a thinking thing; that is, a mind, or intellect, or understanding, or reason—words of whose meanings I was previously ignorant. Yet I am a true thing and am truly existing; but what kind of thing? I have said it already: a thinking thing.

What else am I? I will set my imagination in motion. I am not that concatenation of members we call the human body. Neither am I even some subtle air infused into these members, nor a wind, nor a fire, nor a vapor, nor a breath, nor anything I devise for myself. For I have supposed these things to be nothing. The assumption still stands; yet nevertheless I am something. But is it perhaps the case that these very things which I take to be nothing, because they are unknown to me, nevertheless are in fact no different from that "me" that I know? This I do not know, and I will not quarrel about it now. I can make a judgment only about things that are known to me. I know that I exist; I ask now who is this "I" whom I know? Most certainly, in the strict sense the knowledge of this "I" does not depend upon things of whose existence I do not yet have knowledge. Therefore it is not dependent upon any of those things that I simulate in my imagination. But this word "simulate" warns me of my error. For I would indeed be simulating were I to "imagine" that I was something, because imagining is merely the contemplating of the shape or image of a corporeal thing. But I now know with certainty that I am and also that all these images—and, generally, everything belonging to the nature of the body—could turn out to be nothing but dreams. Once I have realized this, I would seem to be speaking no less foolishly were I to say: "I will use my imagination in order to recognize more distinctly who I am," than were I to say: "Now I surely am awake, and I see something true; but since I do not yet see it clearly enough, I will deliberately fall asleep so that my dreams might represent it to me more truly and more clearly." Thus I realize that none of what I can grasp by means of the imagination pertains to this knowledge that I have of myself. Moreover, I realize that I must be most diligent about withdrawing my mind from these things so that it can perceive its nature as distinctly as possible.

But what then am I? A thing that thinks. What is that? A thing that doubts, understands, affirms, denies, wills, refuses, and that also imagines and senses.

Indeed it is no small matter if all of these things belong to me. But why should they not belong to me? Is it not the very same "I" who now doubts almost everything, who nevertheless understands something, who affirms that this one thing is true, who denies other things, who desires to know more, who wishes not to be deceived, who imagines many things even against my will, who also notices many things which appear to come from the senses? What is there in all of this that is not every bit as true as the fact that I exist—even if I am always asleep or even if my creator makes every effort to mislead me? Which of these things is distinct from my thought? Which of them can be said to be separate from myself? For it is so obvious that it is I who doubt, I who understand, and I who will, that there is nothing by which it could be explained more clearly. But indeed it is also the same "I" who imagines; for although perhaps, as I supposed before, absolutely nothing that I imagined is true, still the very power of imagining really does exist, and constitutes a part of my thought. Finally, it is this same "I" who senses or who is cognizant of bodily things as if through the senses. For example, I now see a light, I hear a noise, I feel heat. These things are false, since I am asleep. Yet I certainly do seem to see, hear, and feel warmth. This cannot be false. Properly speaking, this is what in me is called "sensing." But this, precisely so taken, is nothing other than thinking.

From these considerations I am beginning to know a little better what I am. But it still seems (and I cannot resist believing) that corporeal things—whose images are formed by thought, and which the senses themselves examine—are much more distinctly known than this mysterious "I" which does not fall within the imagination. And yet it would be strange indeed were I to grasp the very things I consider to be doubtful, unknown, and foreign to me more distinctly than what is true, what is known—than, in short, myself. But I see what is happening: my mind loves to wander and does not yet permit itself to be restricted within the confines of truth. So be it then; let us just this once allow it completely free rein, so that, a little while later, when the time has come to pull in the reins, the mind may more readily permit itself to be controlled.

Let us consider those things which are commonly believed to be the most distinctly grasped of all: namely the bodies we touch and see. Not bodies in general, mind you, for these general perceptions are apt to be somewhat more confused, but one body in particular. Let us take, for instance, this piece of wax. It has been taken quite recently from the honeycomb; it has not yet lost all the honey flavor. It retains some of the scent of the flowers from which it was collected. Its color, shape, and size are manifest. It is hard and cold; it is easy to touch. If you rap on it with your knuckle it will emit a sound. In short, everything is present in it that appears needed to enable a body to be known as distinctly as possible. But notice that, as I am speaking, I am bringing it close to the fire. The remaining traces of the honey flavor are disappearing; the scent is vanishing; the color is changing; the original shape is disappearing. Its size is increasing; it is becoming liquid and hot; you can hardly touch it. And now, when you rap on it, it no longer emits any sound. Does the same wax still remain? I must confess that it does; no one denies it; no one thinks otherwise. So what was there in the wax that was so distinctly grasped? Certainly none of the aspects that I reached by means of the senses. For whatever came under the senses of taste, smell, sight, touch or hearing has now changed; and yet the wax remains.

Perhaps the wax was what I now think it is: namely that the wax itself never really was the sweetness of the honey, nor the fragrance of the flowers, nor the whiteness, nor the shape, nor the sound, but instead was a body that a short time ago manifested itself to me in these ways, and now does so in other ways. But just what precisely is this thing that I thus imagine? Let us focus our attention on this and see what remains after we have removed everything that does not belong to the wax: only that it is something extended, flexible, and mutable. But what is it to be flexible and mutable? Is it what my imagination shows it to be: namely, that this piece of wax can change from a round to a square shape, or from the latter to a triangular shape? Not at all; for I grasp that the wax is capable of innumerable changes of this sort, even though I am incapable of running through these innumerable changes by using my imagination. Therefore this insight is not achieved by the faculty of imagination. What is it to be extended? Is this thing's extension also unknown? For it becomes greater in wax that is beginning to melt, greater in boiling wax, and greater still as the heat is increased. And I would not judge correctly what the wax is if I did not believe that it takes on an even greater variety of dimensions than I could ever grasp with the imagination. It remains then for me to concede that I do not grasp what this wax is through the imagination; rather, I perceive it through the mind alone. The point I am making refers to this particular piece of wax, for the case of wax in general is clearer still. But what is this piece of wax which is perceived only by the mind? Surely it is the same piece of wax that I see, touch, and imagine; in short it is the same piece of wax I took it to be from the very beginning. But I need to realize that the perception of the wax is neither a seeing, nor a touching, nor an imagining. Nor has it ever been, even though it previously seemed so; rather it is an inspection on the part of the mind alone. This inspection can be imperfect and confused, as it was before, or clear and distinct, as it is now, depending on how closely I pay attention to the things in which the piece of wax consists.

But meanwhile I marvel at how prone my mind is to errors. For although I am considering these things within myself silently and without words, nevertheless I seize upon words themselves and I am nearly deceived by the ways in which people commonly speak. For we say that we see the wax itself, if it is present, and not that we judge it to be present from its color or shape. Whence I might conclude straightaway that I know the wax through the vision had by the eye, and not through an inspection on the part of the mind alone. But then were I perchance to look out my window and observe men crossing the square, I would ordinarily say I see the men themselves just as I say I see the wax. But what do I see aside from hats and clothes, which could conceal automata? Yet I judge them to be men. Thus what I thought I had seen with my eyes, I actually grasped solely with the faculty of judgment, which is in my mind.

But a person who seeks to know more than the common crowd ought to be ashamed of himself for looking for doubt in common ways of speaking. Let us then go forward and inquire when it was that I perceived more perfectly and evidently what the piece of wax was. Was it when I first saw it and believed I knew it by the external sense, or at least by the so-called common sense, that is, the power of imagination? Or do I have more perfect knowledge now, when I have diligently examined both what the wax is and how it is known? Surely it is absurd to be in doubt about this matter. For what was there in my initial perception that was distinct? What was there that any animal seemed incapable of possessing? But indeed when I distinguish the wax from its external forms, as if stripping it of its clothing, and look at the wax in its nakedness, then, even though there can be still an error in my judgment, nevertheless I cannot perceive it thus without a human mind.

But what am I to say about this mind, that is, about myself? For as yet I admit nothing else to be in me over and above the mind. What, I ask, am I who seem to perceive this wax so distinctly? Do I not know myself not only much more truly and with greater certainty, but also much more distinctly and evidently? For if I judge that the wax exists from the fact that I see it, certainly from this same fact that I see the wax it follows much more evidently that I myself exist. For it could happen that what I see is not truly wax. It could happen that I have no eyes with which to see anything. But it is utterly impossible that, while I see or think I see (I do not now distinguish these two), I who think am not something. Likewise, if I judge that the wax exists from the fact that I touch it, the same outcome will again obtain, namely that I exist. If I judge that the wax exists from the fact that I imagine it, or for any other reason, plainly the same thing follows. But what I note regarding the wax applies to everything else that is external to me. Furthermore, if my perception of the wax seemed more distinct after it became known to me not only on account of sight or touch, but on account of many reasons, one has to admit how much more distinctly I am now known to myself. For there is not a single consideration that can aid in my perception of the wax or of any other body that fails to make even more manifest the nature of my mind. But there are still so many other things in the mind itself on the basis of which my knowledge of it can be rendered more distinct that it hardly seems worth enumerating those things which emanate to it from the body.

But lo and behold, I have returned on my own to where I wanted to be. For since I now know that even bodies are not, properly speaking, perceived by the senses or by the faculty of imagination, but by the intellect alone, and that they are not perceived through their being touched or seen, but only through their being understood, I manifestly know that nothing can be perceived more easily and more evidently than my own mind. But since the tendency to hang on to long-held beliefs cannot be put aside so quickly, I want to stop here, so that by the length of my meditation this new knowledge may be more deeply impressed upon my memory.

MEDITATION THREE: Concerning God, That He Exists

I will now shut my eyes, stop up my ears, and withdraw all my senses. I will also blot out from my thoughts all images of corporeal things, or rather, since the latter is hardly possible, I will regard these images as empty, false and worthless. And as I converse with myself alone and look more deeply into myself, I will attempt to render myself gradually better known and more familiar to myself. I am a thing that thinks, that is to say, a thing that doubts, affirms, denies, understands a few things, is ignorant of many things, wills, refrains from willing, and also imagines and senses. For as I observed earlier, even though these things that I sense or imagine may perhaps be nothing at all outside me, nevertheless I am certain that these modes of thinking, which are cases of what I call sensing and imagining, insofar as they are merely modes of thinking, do exist within me.

In these few words, I have reviewed everything I truly know, or at least what so far I have noticed that I know. Now I will ponder more carefully to see whether perhaps there may be other things belonging to me that up until now I have failed to notice. I am certain that I am a thinking thing. But do I not therefore also know what is required for me to be certain of anything? Surely in this first instance of knowledge, there is nothing but a certain clear and distinct perception of what I affirm. Yet this would hardly be enough to render me certain of the truth of a thing, if it could ever happen that something that I perceived so clearly and distinctly were false. And thus I now seem able to posit as a general rule that everything I very clearly and distinctly perceive is true.

Be that as it may, I have previously admitted many things as wholly certain and evident that nevertheless I later discovered to be doubtful. What sort of things were these? Why, the earth, the sky, the stars, and all the other things I perceived by means of the senses. But what was it about these things that I clearly perceived? Surely the fact that the ideas or thoughts of these things were hovering before my mind. But even now I do not deny that these ideas are in me. Yet there was something else I used to affirm, which, owing to my habitual tendency to believe it, I used to think was something I clearly perceived, even though I actually did not perceive it at all: namely, that certain things existed outside me, things from which those ideas proceeded and which those ideas completely resembled. But on this point I was mistaken; or rather, if my judgment was a true one, it was not the result of the force of my perception.

But what about when I considered something very simple and easy in the areas of arithmetic or geometry, for example that two plus three make five, and the like? Did I not intuit them at least clearly enough so as to affirm them as true? To be sure, I did decide later on that I must doubt these things, but that was only because it occurred to me that some God could perhaps have given me a nature such that I might be deceived even

Meditation Three

about matters that seemed most evident. But whenever this preconceived opinion about the supreme power of God occurs to me, I cannot help admitting that, were he to wish it, it would be easy for him to cause me to err even in those matters that I think I intuit as clearly as possible with the eyes of the mind. On the other hand, whenever I turn my attention to those very things that I think I perceive with such great clarity, I am so completely persuaded by them that I spontaneously blurt out these words: "let anyone who can do so deceive me; so long as I think that I am something, he will never bring it about that I am nothing. Nor will he one day make it true that I never existed, for it is true now that I do exist. Nor will he even bring it about that perhaps two plus three might equal more or less than five, or similar items in which I recognize an obvious contradiction." And certainly, because I have no reason for thinking that there is a God who is a deceiver (and of course I do not yet sufficiently know whether there even is a God), the basis for doubting, depending as it does merely on the above hypothesis, is very tenuous and, so to speak, metaphysical. But in order to remove even this basis for doubt, I should at the first opportunity inquire whether there is a God, and, if there is, whether or not he can be a deceiver. For if I am ignorant of this, it appears I am never capable of being completely certain about anything else.

However, at this stage good order seems to demand that I first group all my thoughts into certain classes, and ask in which of them truth or falsity properly resides. Some of these thoughts are like images of things; to these alone does the word "idea" properly apply, as when I think of a man, or a chimera, or the sky, or an angel, or God. Again there are other thoughts that take different forms: for example, when I will, or fear, or affirm, or deny, there is always some thing that I grasp as the subject of my thought, yet I embrace in my thought something more than the likeness of that thing. Some of these thoughts are called volitions or affects, while others are called judgments.

Now as far as ideas are concerned, if they are considered alone and in their own right, without being referred to something else, they cannot, properly speaking, be false. For whether it is a she-goat or a chimera that I am imagining, it is no less true that I imagine the one than the other. Moreover, we need not fear that there is falsity in the will itself or in the affects, for although I can choose evil things or even things that are utterly non-existent, I cannot conclude from this that it is untrue that I do choose these things. Thus there remain only judgments in which I must take care not to be mistaken. Now the principal and most frequent error to be found in judgments consists in the fact that I judge that the ideas which are in me are similar to or in conformity with certain things outside me. Obviously, if I were to consider these ideas merely as certain modes of my thought, and were not to refer them to anything else, they could hardly give me any subject matter for error.

Among these ideas, some appear to me to be innate, some adventitious, and some produced by me. For I understand what a thing is, what truth is, what thought is, and I appear to have derived this exclusively from my very own nature. But say I am now hearing a noise, or looking at the sun, or feeling the fire; up until now I judged that these things proceeded from certain things outside me, and finally, that sirens, hippogriffs, and the like are made by me. Or perhaps I can even think of all these ideas as being adventitious, or as being innate, or as fabrications, for I have not yet clearly ascertained their true origin.

But here I must inquire particularly into those ideas that I believe to be derived from things existing outside me. Just what reason do I have for believing that these ideas resemble those things? Well, I do seem to have been so taught by nature. Moreover, I do know from experience that these ideas do not depend upon my will, nor consequently upon myself, for I often notice them even against my will. Now, for example, whether or not I will it, I feel heat. It is for this reason that I believe this feeling or idea of heat comes to me from something other than myself, namely from the heat of the fire by which I am sitting. Nothing is more obvious than the judgment that this thing is sending its likeness rather than something else into me.

I will now see whether these reasons are powerful enough. When I say here "I have been so taught by nature," all I have in mind is that I am driven by a spontaneous impulse to believe this, and not that some light of nature is showing me that it is true. These are two very different things. For whatever is shown me by this light of nature, for example, that from the fact that I doubt, it follows that I am, and the like, cannot in any way be doubtful. This is owing to the fact that there can be no other faculty that I can trust as much as this light and which could teach that these things are not true. But as far as natural impulses are concerned, in the past I have often judged myself to have been driven by them to make the poorer choice when it was a question of choosing a good; and I fail to see why I should place any greater faith in them than in other matters.

Again, although these ideas do not depend upon my will, it does not follow that they necessarily proceed from things existing outside me. For just as these impulses about which I spoke just now seem to be different from my will, even though they are in me, so too perhaps there is also in me some other faculty, one not yet sufficiently known to me, which produces these ideas, just as it has always seemed up to now that ideas are formed in me without any help from external things when I am asleep.

And finally, even if these ideas did proceed from things other than myself, it does not therefore follow that they must resemble those things. Indeed it seems I have frequently noticed a vast difference in many respects. For example, I find within myself two distinct ideas of the sun. One idea is drawn, as it were, from the senses. Now it is this idea which, of all those that I take to be derived from outside me, is most in need of examination. By means of this idea the sun appears to me to be quite small. But there is another idea, one derived from astronomical reasoning, that is, it is elicited from certain notions that are innate in me, or else is fashioned by me in some other way. Through this idea the sun is shown to be several times larger than the earth. Both ideas surely cannot resemble the same sun existing outside me; and reason convinces me that the idea that seems to have emanated from the sun itself from so close is the very one that least resembles the sun.

All these points demonstrate sufficiently that up to this point it was not a well-founded judgment but only a blind impulse that formed the basis of my belief that things existing outside me send ideas or images of themselves to me through the sense organs or by some other means.

But still another way occurs to me for inquiring whether some of the things of which there are ideas in me do exist outside me: insofar as these ideas are merely modes of thought, I see no inequality among them; they all seem to proceed from me in the same manner. But insofar as one idea represents one thing and another idea another thing, it is obvious that they do differ very greatly from one another. Unquestionably, those ideas that display substances to me are something more and, if I may say so, contain within themselves more objective reality than those which represent only modes or accidents. Again, the idea that enables me to understand a supreme deity, eternal, infinite, omniscient, omnipotent, and creator of all things other than himself, clearly has more objective reality within it than do those ideas through which finite substances are displayed.

Now it is indeed evident by the light of nature that there must be at least as much [reality] in the efficient and total cause as there is in the effect of that same cause. For whence, I ask, could an effect get its reality, if not from its cause? And how could the cause give that reality to the effect, unless it also possessed that reality? Hence it follows that something cannot come into being out of nothing, and also that what is more perfect (that is, what contains in itself more reality) cannot come into being from what is less perfect. But this is manifestly true not merely for those effects whose reality is actual or formal, but also for ideas in which only objective reality is considered. For example, not only can a stone which did not exist previously not now begin to exist unless it is produced by something in which there is, either formally or eminently, everything that is in the stone; nor heat be introduced into a subject which was not already hot unless it is done by something that is of at least as perfect an order as heat—and the same for the rest—but it is also true that there can be in me no idea of heat, or of a stone, unless it is placed in me by some cause that has at least as much reality as I conceive to be in the heat or in the stone. For although this cause conveys none of its actual or formal reality to my idea, it should not be thought for that reason that it must be less real. Rather, the very nature of an idea is such that of itself it needs no formal reality other than what it borrows from my thought, of which it is a mode. But that a particular idea contains this as opposed to that objective reality is surely owing to some cause in which there is at least as much formal reality as there is objective reality contained in the idea. For if we assume that something is found in the idea that was not in its cause, then the idea gets that something from nothing. Yet as imperfect a mode of being as this is by which a thing exists in the intellect objectively through an idea, nevertheless it is plainly not nothing; hence it cannot get its being from nothing.

Moreover, even though the reality that I am considering in my ideas is merely objective reality, I ought not on that account to suspect that there is no need for the same reality to be formally in the causes of these ideas, but that it suffices for it to be in them objectively. For just as the objective mode of being belongs to ideas by their very nature, so the formal mode of being belongs to the causes of ideas, at least to the first and preeminent ones, by their very nature. And although one idea can perhaps issue from another, nevertheless no infinite regress is permitted here; eventually some first idea must be reached whose cause is a sort of archetype that contains formally all the reality that is in the idea merely objectively. Thus it is clear to me by the light of nature that the ideas that are in me are like images that can easily fail to match the perfection of the things from which they have been drawn, but which can contain nothing greater or more perfect.

And the longer and more attentively I examine all these points, the more clearly and distinctly I know they are true. But what am I ultimately to conclude? If the objective reality of any of my ideas is found to be so great that I am certain that the same reality was not in me, either formally or eminently, and that therefore I myself cannot be the cause of the idea, then it necessarily follows that I am not alone in the world, but that something else, which is the cause of this idea, also exists. But if no such idea is found in me, I will have no argument whatsoever to make me certain of the existence of anything other than myself, for I have conscientiously reviewed all these arguments, and so far I have been unable to find any other.

Meditation Three

Among my ideas, in addition to the one that displays me to myself (about which there can be no difficulty at this point), are others that represent God, corporeal and inanimate things, angels, animals, and finally other men like myself.

As to the ideas that display other men, or animals, or angels, I easily understand that they could be fashioned from the ideas that I have of myself, of corporeal things, and of God—even if no men (except myself), no animals, and no angels existed in the world.

As to the ideas of corporeal things, there is nothing in them that is so great that it seems incapable of having originated from me. For if I investigate them thoroughly and examine each one individually in the way I examined the idea of wax yesterday, I notice that there are only a very few things in them that I perceive clearly and distinctly: namely, size, or extension in length, breadth, and depth; shape, which arises from the limits of this extension; position, which various things possessing shape have in relation to one another; and motion, or alteration in position. To these can be added substance, duration, and number. But as for the remaining items, such as light and colors, sounds, odors, tastes, heat and cold and other tactile qualities, I think of these only in a very confused and obscure manner, to the extent that I do not even know whether they are true or false, that is, whether the ideas I have of them are ideas of things or ideas of non-things. For although a short time ago I noted that falsity properly so called (or "formal" falsity) is to be found only in judgments, nevertheless there is another kind of falsity (called "material" falsity) which is found in ideas whenever they represent a non-thing as if it were a thing. For example, the ideas I have of heat and cold fall so far short of being clear and distinct that I cannot tell from them whether cold is merely the privation of heat or whether heat is the privation of cold, or whether both are real qualities, or whether neither is. And because ideas can only be, as it were, of things, if it is true that cold is merely the absence of heat, then an idea that represents cold to me as something real and positive will not inappropriately be called false. The same holds for other similar ideas.

Assuredly I need not assign to these ideas an author distinct from myself. For if they were false, that is, if they were to represent non-things, I know by the light of nature that they proceed from nothing; that is, they are in me for no other reason than that something is lacking in my nature, and that my nature is not entirely perfect. If, on the other hand, these ideas are true, then because they exhibit so little reality to me that I cannot distinguish it from a non-thing, I see no reason why they cannot get their being from me.

As for what is clear and distinct in the ideas of corporeal things, it appears I could have borrowed some of these from the idea of myself: namely, substance, duration, number, and whatever else there may be of this type. For instance, I think that a stone is a substance, that is to say, a thing that is suitable for existing in itself; and likewise I think that I too am a substance. Despite the fact that I conceive myself to be a thinking thing and not an extended thing, whereas I conceive of a stone as an extended thing and not a thinking thing, and hence there is the greatest diversity between these two concepts, nevertheless they seem to agree with one another when considered under the rubric of substance. Furthermore, I perceive that I now exist and recall that I have previously existed for some time. And I have various thoughts and know how many of them there are. It is in doing these things that I acquire the ideas of duration and number, which I can then apply to other things. However, none of the other components out of which the ideas of corporeal things are fashioned (namely extension, shape, position, and motion) are contained in me formally, since I am merely a thinking thing. But since these are only certain modes of a substance, whereas I am a substance, it seems possible that they are contained in me eminently.

Thus there remains only the idea of God. I must consider whether there is anything in this idea that could not have originated from me. I understand by the name "God" a certain substance that is infinite, independent, supremely intelligent and supremely powerful, and that created me along with everything else that exists—if anything else exists. Indeed all these are such that, the more carefully I focus my attention on them, the less possible it seems they could have arisen from myself alone. Thus, from what has been said, I must conclude that God necessarily exists.

For although the idea of substance is in me by virtue of the fact that I am a substance, that fact is not sufficient to explain my having the idea of an infinite substance, since I am finite, unless this idea proceeded from some substance which really was infinite.

Nor should I think that I do not perceive the infinite by means of a true idea, but only through a negation of the finite, just as I perceive rest and darkness by means of a negation of motion and light. On the contrary, I clearly understand that there is more reality in an infinite substance than there is in a finite one. Thus the perception of the infinite is somehow prior in me to the perception of the finite, that is, my perception of God is prior to my perception of myself. For how would I understand that I doubt and that I desire, that is, that I lack something and that I am not wholly perfect, unless there were some idea in me of a more perfect being, by comparison with which I might recognize my defects?

Nor can it be said that this idea of God is perhaps materially false and thus can originate from nothing, as I remarked just now about the ideas of heat and cold, and the like. On the contrary, because it is the most clear and distinct and because it contains more objective reality than any other idea, no idea is in and of itself truer and has less of a basis for being suspected of falsehood. I maintain that this idea of a being that is supremely perfect and infinite is true in the highest degree. For although I could perhaps pretend that such a being does not exist, nevertheless I could not pretend that the idea of such a being discloses to me nothing real, as was the case with the idea of cold which I referred to earlier. It is indeed an idea that is utterly clear and distinct; for whatever I clearly and distinctly perceive to be real and true and to involve some perfection is wholly contained in that idea. It is no objection that I do not comprehend the infinite or that there are countless other things in God that I can in no way either comprehend or perhaps even touch with my thought. For the nature of the infinite is such that it is not comprehended by a being such as I, who am finite. And it is sufficient that I understand this very point and judge that all those things that I clearly perceive and that I know to contain some perfection—and perhaps even countless other things of which I am ignorant—are in God either formally or eminently. The result is that, of all the ideas that are in me, the idea that I have of God is the most true, the most clear and distinct.

But perhaps I am something greater than I myself understand. Perhaps all these perfections that I am attributing to God are somehow in me potentially, although they do no yet assert themselves and are not yet actualized. For I now observe that my knowledge is gradually being increased, and I see nothing standing in the way of its being increased more and more to infinity. Moreover, I see no reason why, with my knowledge thus increased, I could not acquire all the remaining perfections of God. And, finally, if the potential for these perfections is in me already, I see no reason why this potential would not suffice to produce the idea of these perfections.

Yet none of these things can be the case. First, while it is true that my knowledge is gradually being increased and that there are many things in me potentially that are not yet actual, nevertheless, none of these pertains to the idea of God, in which there is nothing whatever that is potential. Indeed this gradual increase is itself a most certain proof of imperfection. Moreover, although my knowledge may always increase more and more, nevertheless I understand that this knowledge will never by this means be actually infinite, because it will never reach a point where it is incapable of greater increase. On the contrary, I judge God to be actually infinite, so that nothing can be added to his perfection. Finally, I perceive that the objective being of an idea cannot be produced by a merely potential being (which, strictly speaking, is nothing), but only by an actual or formal being.

Indeed there is nothing in all these things that is not manifest by the light of nature to one who is conscientious and attentive. But when I am less attentive, and the images of sensible things blind the mind's eye, I do not so easily recall why the idea of a being more perfect than me necessarily proceeds from a being that really is more perfect. This being the case, it is appropriate to ask further whether I myself who have this idea could exist, if such a being did not exist.

From what source, then, do I derive my existence? Why, from myself, or from my parents, or from whatever other things there are that are less perfect than God. For nothing more perfect than God, or even as perfect as God, can be thought or imagined.

But if I got my being from myself, I would not doubt, nor would I desire, nor would I lack anything at all. For I would have given myself all the perfections of which I have some idea; in so doing, I myself would be God! I must not think that the things I lack could perhaps be more difficult to acquire than the ones I have now. On the contrary, it is obvious that it would have been much more difficult for me (that is, a thing or substance that thinks) to emerge out of nothing than it would be to acquire the knowledge of many things about which I am ignorant (these items of knowledge being merely accidents of that substance). Certainly, if I got this greater thing from myself, I would not have denied myself at least those things that can be had more easily. Nor would I have denied myself any of those other things that I perceive to be contained in the idea of God, for surely none of them seem to me more difficult to bring about. But if any of them were more difficult to bring about, they would certainly also seem more difficult to me, even if the remaining ones that I possess I got from myself, since it would be on account of them that I would experience that my power is limited.

Nor am I avoiding the force of these arguments, if I suppose that perhaps I have always existed as I do now, as if it then followed that no author of my existence need be sought. For because the entire span of one's life can be divided into countless parts, each one wholly independent of the rest, it does not follow from the fact that I existed a short time ago that I must exist now, unless some cause, as it were, creates me all over again at this moment, that is to say, which preserves me. For it is obvious to one who pays close attention to the nature of time that plainly the same force and action are needed to preserve anything at each individual moment that it lasts as would be required to create that same thing anew, were it not yet in existence. Thus conservation differs from creation solely by virtue of a distinction of reason; this too is one of those things that are manifest by the light of nature.

Therefore I must now ask myself whether I possess some power by which I can bring it about that I myself, who now exist, will also exist a little later on. For since I am nothing but a thinking thing—or at least since I am now dealing simply and precisely with that part of me which is a thinking thing—if such a power were in me, then I would certainly be aware of it. But I observe that there is no such power; and from this very fact I know most clearly that I depend upon some being other than myself.

But perhaps this being is not God, and I have been produced either by my parents or by some other causes less perfect than God. On the contrary, as I said before, it is obvious that there must be at least as much in the cause as there is in the effect. Thus, regardless of what it is that eventually is assigned as my cause, because I am a thinking thing and have within me a certain idea of God, it must be granted that what caused me is also a thinking thing and it too has an idea of all the perfections which I attribute to God. And I can again inquire of this cause whether it got its existence from itself or from another cause. For if it got its existence from itself, it is evident from what has been said that it is itself God, because, having the power of existing in and of itself, it unquestionably also has the power of actually possessing all the perfections of which it has in itself an idea—that is, all the perfections that I conceive to be in God. However, if it got its existence from another cause, I will once again inquire in similar fashion about this other cause: whether it got its existence from itself or from another cause, until finally I arrive at the ultimate cause, which will be God. For it is apparent enough that there can be no infinite regress here, especially since I am not dealing here merely with the cause that once produced me, but also and most especially with the cause that preserves me at the present time.

Nor can one fancy that perhaps several partial causes have concurred in bringing me into being, and that I have taken the ideas of the various perfections I attribute to God from a variety of causes, so that all of these perfections are found somewhere in the universe, but not all joined together in a single being—God. On the contrary, the unity, the simplicity, that is, the inseparability of all those features that are in God is one of the chief perfections that I understand to be in him. Certainly the idea of the unity of all his perfections could not have been placed in me by any cause from which I did not also get the ideas of the other perfections; for neither could some cause have made me understand them joined together and inseparable from one another, unless it also caused me to recognize what they were.

Finally, as to my parents, even if everything that I ever believed about them were true, still it is certainly not they who preserve me; nor is it they who in any way brought me into being, insofar as I am a thinking thing. Rather, they merely placed certain dispositions in the matter which I judged to contain me, that is, a mind, which now is the only thing I take myself to be. And thus there can be no difficulty here concerning my parents. Indeed I have no choice but to conclude that the mere fact of my existing and of there being in me an idea of a most perfect being, that is, God, demonstrates most evidently that God too exists.

All that remains for me is to ask how I received this idea of God. For I did not draw it from the senses; it never came upon me unexpectedly, as is usually the case with the ideas of sensible things when these things present themselves (or seem to present themselves) to the external sense organs. Nor was it made by me, for I plainly can neither subtract anything from it nor add anything to it. Thus the only option remaining is that this idea is innate in me, just as the idea of myself is innate in me.

To be sure, it is not astonishing that in creating me, God should have endowed me with this idea, so that it would be like the mark of the craftsman impressed upon his work, although this mark need not be something distinct from the work itself. But the mere fact that God created me makes it highly plausible that I have somehow been made in his image and likeness, and that I perceive this likeness, in which the idea of God is contained, by means of the same faculty by which I perceive myself. That is, when I turn the mind's eye toward myself, I understand not only that I am something incomplete and dependent upon another, something aspiring indefinitely for greater and greater or better things, but also that the being on whom I depend has in himself all those greater things—not merely indefinitely and potentially, but infinitely and actually, and thus that he is God. The whole force of the argument rests on the fact that I recognize that it would be impossible for me to exist, being of such a nature as I am (namely, having in me the idea of God), unless God did in fact exist. God, I say, that same being the idea of whom is in me: a being having all those perfections that I cannot comprehend, but can somehow touch with my thought, and a being subject to no defects whatever. From these considerations it is quite obvious that he cannot be a deceiver, for it is manifest by the light of nature that all fraud and deception depend on some defect.

But before examining this idea more closely and at the same time inquiring into other truths that can be gathered from it, at this point I want to spend some time contemplating this God, to ponder his attributes and, so far as the eye of my darkened mind can take me, to gaze upon, to admire, and to adore the beauty of this immense light. For just as we believe by faith that the greatest felicity of the next life consists solely in this contemplation of the divine majesty, so too we now experience that from the same contemplation, although it is much less perfect, the greatest pleasure of which we are capable in this life can be perceived.

MEDITATION FOUR: Concerning the True and the False

Lately I have become accustomed to withdrawing my mind from the senses, and I have carefully taken note of the fact that very few things are truly perceived regarding corporeal things, although a great many more things are known regarding the human mind, and still many more things regarding God. The upshot is that I now have no difficulty directing my thought away from things that can be imagined to things that can be grasped only by the understanding and are wholly separate from matter. In fact the idea I clearly have of the human mind—insofar as it is a thinking thing, not extended in length, breadth or depth, and having nothing else from the body—is far more distinct than the idea of any corporeal thing. And when I take note of the fact that I doubt, or that I am a thing that is incomplete and dependent, there comes to mind a clear and distinct idea of a being that is independent and complete, that is, an idea of God. And from the mere fact that such an idea is in me, or that I who have this idea exist, I draw the obvious conclusion that God also exists, and that my existence depends entirely upon him at each and every moment. This conclusion is so obvious that I am confident that the human mind can know nothing more evident or more certain. And now I seem to see a way by which I might progress from this contemplation of the true God, in whom, namely, are hidden all the treasures of the sciences and wisdom, to the knowledge of other things.

To begin with, I acknowledge that it is impossible for God ever to deceive me, for trickery or deception is always indicative of some imperfection. And although the ability to deceive seems to be an indication of cleverness or power, the will to deceive undoubtedly attests to maliciousness or weakness. Accordingly, deception is incompatible with God.

Next I experience that there is in me a certain faculty of judgment, which, like everything else that is in me, I undoubtedly received from God. And since he does not wish to deceive me, he assuredly has not given me the sort of faculty with which I could ever make a mistake, when I use it properly.

No doubt regarding this matter would remain, but for the fact that it seems to follow from this that I am never capable of making a mistake. For if everything that is in me I got from God, and he gave me no faculty for making mistakes, it seems I am incapable of ever erring. And thus, so long as I think exclusively about God and focus my attention exclusively on him, I discern no cause of error or falsity. But once I turn my attention back on myself, I nevertheless experience that I am subject to countless errors. As I seek a cause of these errors, I notice that passing before me is not only a real and positive idea of God (that is, of a supremely perfect being), but also, as it were, a certain negative idea of nothingness (that is, of what is at the greatest possible distance from any perfection), and that I have been so constituted as a kind of middle ground between God and nothingness, or between the supreme being and non-being. Thus insofar as I have been created by the supreme being, there is nothing in me by means of which I might be deceived or be led into error; but insofar as I participate in nothingness or non-being, that is, insofar as I am not the supreme being and lack a great many things, it is not surprising that I make mistakes. Thus I certainly understand that error as such is not something real that depends upon God, but rather is merely a defect. And thus there is no need to account for my errors by positing a faculty given to me by God for this purpose. Rather, it just so happens that I make mistakes because the faculty of judging the truth, which I got from God, is not, in my case, infinite.

55   Still this is not yet altogether satisfactory; for error is not a pure negation, but rather a privation or a lack of some knowledge that somehow ought to be in me. And when I attend to the nature of God, it seems impossible that he would have placed in me a faculty that is not perfect in its kind or that is lacking some perfection it ought to have. For if it is true that the more expert the craftsman, the more perfect the works he produces, what can that supreme creator of all things make that is not perfect in all respects? No doubt God could have created me such that I never erred. No doubt, again, God always wills what is best. Is it then better that I should be in error rather than not?

As I mull these things over more carefully, it occurs to me first that there is no reason to marvel at the fact that God should bring about certain things the reasons for which I do not understand. Nor is his existence therefore to be doubted because I happen to experience other things of which I fail to grasp why and how he made them. For since I know now that my nature is very weak and limited, whereas the nature of God is immense, incomprehensible, and infinite, this is sufficient for me also to know that he can make innumerable things whose causes escape me. For this reason alone the entire class of causes which people customarily derive from a thing's "end," I judge to be utterly useless in physics. It is not without rashness that I think myself capable of inquiring into the ends of God.

It also occurs to me that whenever we ask whether the works of God

Meditation Four

are perfect, we should keep in view not simply some one creature in isolation from the rest, but the universe as a whole. For perhaps something might rightfully appear very imperfect if it were all by itself, and yet be most perfect, to the extent that it has the status of a part in the universe. And although subsequent to having decided to doubt everything, I have come to know with certainty only that I and God exist, nevertheless, after having taken note of the immense power of God, I cannot deny that many other things have been made by him, or at least could have been made by him. Thus I may have the status of a part in the universal scheme of things.

56

Next, as I focus more closely on myself and inquire into the nature of my errors (the only things that are indicative of some imperfection in me), I note that these errors depend on the simultaneous concurrence of two causes: the faculty of knowing that is in me and the faculty of choosing, that is, the free choice of the will, in other words, simultaneously on the intellect and will. Through the intellect alone I merely perceive ideas, about which I can render a judgment. Strictly speaking, no error is to be found in the intellect when properly viewed in this manner. For although perhaps there may exist countless things about which I have no idea, nevertheless it must not be said that, strictly speaking, I am deprived of these ideas but only that I lack them in a negative sense. This is because I cannot adduce an argument to prove that God ought to have given me a greater faculty of knowing than he did. No matter how expert a craftsman I understand him to be, still I do not for that reason believe he ought to have bestowed on each one of his works all the perfections that he can put into some. Nor, on the other hand, can I complain that the will or free choice I have received from God is insufficiently ample or perfect, since I experience that it is limited by no boundaries whatever. In fact, it seems to be especially worth noting that no other things in me are so perfect or so great but that I understand that they can be still more perfect or greater. If, for example, I consider the faculty of understanding, I immediately recognize that in my case it is very small and quite limited, and at the very same time I form an idea of another much greater faculty of understanding—in fact, an understanding which is consummately great and infinite; and from the fact that I can form an idea of this faculty, I perceive that it pertains to the nature of God. Similarly, were I to examine the faculty of memory or imagination, or any of the other faculties, I would understand that in my case each of these is without exception feeble and limited, whereas in the case of God I understand each faculty to be boundless. It is only the will or free choice that I experience to be so great in me that I cannot grasp the idea of any greater faculty. This is so much the case that the will is the chief basis for my understanding

57

that I bear a certain image and likeness of God. For although the faculty of willing is incomparably greater in God than it is in me, both by virtue of the knowledge and power that are joined to it and that render it more resolute and efficacious and by virtue of its object inasmuch as the divine will stretches over a greater number of things, nevertheless, when viewed in itself formally and precisely, God's faculty of willing does not appear to be any greater. This is owing to the fact that willing is merely a matter of being able to do or not do the same thing, that is, of being able to affirm or deny, to pursue or to shun; or better still, the will consists solely in the fact that when something is proposed to us by our intellect either to affirm or deny, to pursue or to shun, we are moved in such a way that we sense that we are determined to it by no external force. In order to be free I need not be capable of being moved in each direction; on the contrary, the more I am inclined toward one direction—either because I clearly understand that there is in it an aspect of the good and the true, or because God has thus disposed the inner recesses of my thought—the more freely do I choose that direction. Nor indeed does divine grace or natural knowledge ever diminish one's freedom; rather, they increase and strengthen it. However, the indifference that I experience when there is no reason moving me more in one direction than in another is the lowest grade of freedom; it is indicative not of any perfection in freedom, but rather of a defect, that is, a certain negation in knowledge. Were I always to see clearly what is true and good, I would never deliberate about what is to be judged or chosen. In that event, although I would be entirely free, I could never be indifferent.

But from these considerations I perceive that the power of willing, which I got from God, is not, taken by itself, the cause of my errors, for it is most ample as well as perfect in its kind. Nor is my power of understanding the cause of my errors. For since I got my power of understanding from God, whatever I understand I doubtless understand rightly, and it is impossible for me to be deceived in this. What then is the source of my errors? They are owing simply to the fact that, since the will extends further than the intellect, I do not contain the will within the same boundaries; rather, I also extend it to things I do not understand. Because the will is indifferent in regard to such matters, it easily turns away from the true and the good; and in this way I am deceived and I sin.

For example, during these last few days I was examining whether anything in the world exists, and I noticed that, from the very fact that I was making this examination, it obviously followed that I exist. Nevertheless, I could not help judging that what I understood so clearly was true; not that I was coerced into making this judgment because of some external force, but because a great light in my intellect gave way to a great inclination in my will, and the less indifferent I was, the more spontaneously and freely did I believe it. But now, in addition to my knowing that I exist, insofar as I am a certain thinking thing, I also observe a certain idea of corporeal nature. It happens that I am in doubt as to whether the thinking nature which is in me, or rather which I am, is something different from this corporeal nature, or whether both natures are one and the same thing. And I assume that as yet no consideration has occurred to my intellect to convince me of the one alternative rather than the other. Certainly in virtue of this very fact I am indifferent about whether to affirm or to deny either alternative, or even whether to make no judgment at all in the matter.

Moreover, this indifference extends not merely to things about which the intellect knows absolutely nothing, but extends generally to everything of which the intellect does not have a clear enough knowledge at the very time when the will is deliberating on them. For although probable guesses may pull me in one direction, the mere knowledge that they are only guesses and not certain and indubitable proofs is all it takes to push my assent in the opposite direction. These last few days have provided me with ample experience on this point. For all the beliefs that I had once held to be most true I have supposed to be utterly false, and for the sole reason that I determined that I could somehow raise doubts about them.

But if I hold off from making a judgment when I do not perceive what is true with sufficient clarity and distinctness, it is clear that I am acting properly and am not committing an error. But if instead I were to make an assertion or a denial, then I am not using my freedom properly. Were I to select the alternative that is false, then obviously I will be in error. But were I to embrace the other alternative, it will be by sheer luck that I happen upon the truth; but I will still not be without fault, for it is manifest by the light of nature that a perception on the part of the intellect must always precede a determination on the part of the will. Inherent in this incorrect use of free will is the privation that constitutes the very essence of error: the privation, I say, present in this operation insofar as the operation proceeds from me, but not in the faculty given to me by God, nor even in its operation insofar as it depends upon him.

Indeed I have no cause for complaint on the grounds that God has not given me a greater power of understanding or a greater light of nature than he has, for it is of the essence of a finite intellect not to understand many things, and it is of the essence of a created intellect to be finite. Actually, instead of thinking that he has withheld from me or deprived me of those things that he has not given me, I ought to thank God, who never owed me anything, for what he has bestowed upon me.

Again, I have no cause for complaint on the grounds that God has given me a will that has a wider scope than my intellect. For since the will consists of merely one thing, something indivisible, as it were, it does not seem that its nature could withstand anything being removed from it. Indeed, the more ample the will is, the more I ought to thank the one who gave it to me.

Finally, I should not complain because God concurs with me in eliciting those acts of the will, that is those judgments, in which I am mistaken. For insofar as those acts depend on God, they are absolutely true and good; and in a certain sense, there is greater perfection in me in being able to elicit those acts than in not being able to do so. But privation, in which alone the defining characteristic of falsehood and wrong-doing is to be found, has no need whatever for God's concurrence, since a privation is not a thing, nor, when it is related to God as its cause, is it to be called a privation, but simply a negation. For it is surely no imperfection in God that he has given me the freedom to give or withhold my assent in those instances where he has not placed a clear and distinct perception in my intellect. But surely it is an imperfection in me that I do not use my freedom well and that I make judgments about things I do not properly understand. Nevertheless, I see that God could easily have brought it about that, while still being free and having finite knowledge, I should nonetheless never make a mistake. This result could have been achieved either by his endowing my intellect with a clear and distinct perception of everything about which I would ever deliberate, or by simply impressing the following rule so firmly upon my memory that I could never forget it: I should never judge anything that I do not clearly and distinctly understand. I readily understand that, considered as a totality, I would have been more perfect than I am now, had God made me that way. But I cannot therefore deny that it may somehow be a greater perfection in the universe as a whole that some of its parts are not immune to error, while others are, than if all of them were exactly alike. And I have no right to complain that the part God has wished me to play is not the principal and most perfect one of all.

Furthermore, even if I cannot abstain from errors in the first way mentioned above, which depends upon a clear perception of everything about which I must deliberate, nevertheless I can avoid error in the other way, which depends solely on my remembering to abstain from making judgments whenever the truth of a given matter is not apparent. For although I experience a certain infirmity in myself, namely that I am unable to keep my attention constantly focused on one and the same item of knowledge, nevertheless, by attentive and often repeated meditation, I can bring it about that I call this rule to mind whenever the situation calls for it, and thus I would acquire a certain habit of not erring.

Since herein lies the greatest and chief perfection of man, I think today's meditation, in which I investigated the cause of error and falsity, was quite profitable. Nor can this cause be anything other than the one I have described; for as often as I restrain my will when I make judgments, so that it extends only to those matters that the intellect clearly and distinctly discloses to it, it plainly cannot happen that I err. For every clear and distinct perception is surely something, and hence it cannot come from nothing. On the contrary, it must necessarily have God for its author: God, I say, that supremely perfect being to whom it is repugnant to be a deceiver. Therefore the perception is most assuredly true. Today I have learned not merely what I must avoid so as never to make a mistake, but at the same time what I must do to attain truth. For I will indeed attain it, if only I pay enough attention to all the things that I perfectly understand, and separate them off from the rest, which I apprehend more confusedly and more obscurely. I will be conscientious about this in the future.

Meditation Five: Concerning the Essence of Material Things, and Again Concerning God, That He Exists

Several matters remain for me to examine concerning the attributes of God and myself, that is, concerning the nature of my mind. But perhaps I will take these up at some other time. For now, since I have noted what to avoid and what to do in order to attain the truth, nothing seems more pressing than that I try to free myself from the doubts into which I fell a few days ago, and that I see whether anything certain is to be had concerning material things.

Yet, before inquiring whether any such things exist outside me, I surely ought to consider the ideas of these things, insofar as they exist in my thought, and see which ones are distinct and which ones are confused.

I do indeed distinctly imagine the quantity that philosophers commonly call "continuous," that is, the extension of this quantity, or rather of the thing quantified in length, breadth and depth. I enumerate the various parts in it. I ascribe to these parts any sizes, shapes, positions, and local movements whatever; to these movements I ascribe any durations whatever.

Not only are these things manifestly known and transparent to me, viewed thus in a general way, but also, when I focus my attention on them, I perceive countless particulars concerning shapes, number, movement, and the like. Their truth is so open and so much in accord with my nature that, when I first discover them, it seems I am not so much learning something new as recalling something I knew beforehand. In other words, it seems as though I am noticing things for the first time that were in fact in me for a long while, although I had not previously directed a mental gaze upon them.

What I believe must be considered above all here is the fact that I find within me countless ideas of certain things, that, even if perhaps they do not exist anywhere outside me, still cannot be said to be nothing. And although, in a sense, I think them at will, nevertheless they are not something I have fabricated; rather they have their own true and immutable natures. For example, when I imagine a triangle, even if perhaps no such figure exists outside my thought anywhere in the world and never has, the triangle still has a certain determinate nature, essence, or form which is unchangeable and eternal, which I did not fabricate, and which does not depend on my mind. This is evident from the fact that various properties can be demonstrated regarding this triangle: namely, that its three angles are equal to two right angles, that its longest side is opposite its largest angle, and so on. These are properties I now clearly acknowledge, whether I want to or not, even if I previously had given them no thought whatever when I imagined the triangle. For this reason, then, they were not fabricated by me.

It is irrelevant for me to say that perhaps the idea of a triangle came to me from external things through the sense organs because of course I have on occasion seen triangle-shaped bodies. For I can think of countless other figures, concerning which there can be no suspicion of their ever having entered me through the senses, and yet I can demonstrate various properties of these figures, no less than I can those of the triangle. All these properties are patently true because I know them clearly, and thus they are something and not merely nothing. For it is obvious that whatever is true is something, and I have already demonstrated at some length that all that I know clearly is true. And even if I had not demonstrated this, certainly the nature of my mind is such that nevertheless I cannot refrain from assenting to these things, at least while I perceive them clearly. And I recall that even before now, when I used to keep my attention glued to the objects of the senses, I always took the truths I clearly recognized regarding figures, numbers, or other things pertaining to arithmetic, geometry or, in general, to pure and abstract mathematics to be the most certain of all.

But if, from the mere fact that I can bring forth from my thought the idea of something, it follows that all that I clearly and distinctly perceive to belong to that thing really does belong to it, then cannot this too be a basis for an argument proving the existence of God? Clearly the idea of God, that is, the idea of a supremely perfect being, is one I discover to be no less within me than the idea of any figure or number. And that it belongs to God's nature that he always exists is something I understand no less clearly and distinctly than is the case when I demonstrate in regard to some figure or number that something also belongs to the nature of that figure or number. Thus, even if not everything that I have meditated upon during these last few days were true, still the existence of God ought to have for me at least the same degree of certainty that truths of mathematics had until now.

However, this point is not wholly obvious at first glance, but has a certain look of a sophism about it. Since in all other matters I have become accustomed to distinguishing existence from essence, I easily convince myself that it can even be separated from God's essence, and hence that God can be thought of as not existing. But nevertheless, it is obvious to anyone who pays close attention that existence can no more be separated from God's essence than its having three angles equal to two right angles can be separated from the essence of a triangle, or than that the idea of a valley can be separated from the idea of a mountain. Thus it is no less[1] contradictory to think of God (that is, a supremely perfect being) lacking existence (that is, lacking some perfection) than it is to think of a mountain without a valley.

But granted I can no more think of God as not existing than I can think of a mountain without a valley, nevertheless it surely does not follow from the fact that I think of a mountain with a valley that a mountain exists in the world. Likewise, from the fact that I think of God as existing, it does not seem to follow that God exists, for my thought imposes no necessity on things. And just as one may imagine a winged horse, without there being a horse that has wings, in the same way perhaps I can attach existence to God, even though no God exists.

But there is a sophism lurking here. From the fact that I am unable to think of a mountain without a valley, it does not follow that a mountain or a valley exists anywhere, but only that, whether they exist or not, a mountain and a valley are inseparable from one another. But from the fact that I cannot think of God except as existing, it follows that existence is inseparable from God, and that for this reason he really exists. Not that my thought brings this about or imposes any necessity on anything; but rather the necessity of the thing itself, namely of the existence of God, forces me to think this. For I am not free to think of God without existence, that is, a supremely perfect being without a supreme perfection, as I am to imagine a horse with or without wings.

Further, it should not be said here that even though I surely need to

---

1. A literal translation of the Latin text (*non magis*) is "no more." This is obviously a misstatement on Descartes's part, since it contradicts his own clearly stated views.

assent to the existence of God once I have asserted that God has all perfections and that existence is one of these perfections, nevertheless that earlier assertion need not have been made. Likewise, I need not believe that all four-sided figures can be inscribed in a circle; but given that I posit this, it would then be necessary for me to admit that a rhombus can be inscribed in a circle. Yet this is obviously false. For although it is not necessary that I should ever happen upon any thought of God, nevertheless whenever I am of a mind to think of a being that is first and supreme, and bring forth the idea of God as it were from the storehouse of my mind, I must of necessity ascribe all perfections to him, even if I do not at that time enumerate them all or take notice of each one individually. This necessity plainly suffices so that afterwards, when I realize that existence is a perfection, I rightly conclude that a first and supreme being exists. In the same way, there is no necessity for me ever to imagine a triangle, but whenever I do wish to consider a rectilinear figure having but three angles, I must ascribe to it those properties on the basis of which one rightly infers that the three angles of this figure are no greater than two right angles, even though I do not take note of this at the time. But when I inquire as to the figures that may be inscribed in a circle, there is absolutely no need whatever for my thinking that all four-sided figures are of this sort; for that matter, I cannot even fabricate such a thing, so long as I am of a mind to admit only what I clearly and distinctly understand. Consequently, there is a great difference between false assumptions of this sort and the true ideas that are inborn in me, the first and chief of which is the idea of God. For there are a great many ways in which I understand that this idea is not an invention that is dependent upon my thought, but is an image of a true and immutable nature. First, I cannot think of anything aside from God alone to whose essence existence belongs. Next, I cannot understand how there could be two or more Gods of this kind. Again, once I have asserted that one God now exists, I plainly see that it is necessary that he has existed from eternity and will endure for eternity. Finally, I perceive many other features in God, none of which I can remove or change.

But, whatever type of argument I use, it always comes down to the fact that the only things that fully convince me are those that I clearly and distinctly perceive. And although some of these things I thus perceive are obvious to everyone, while others are discovered only by those who look more closely and inquire carefully, nevertheless, once they have been discovered, they are considered no less certain than the others. For example, in the case of a right triangle, although it is not so readily apparent that the square of the hypotenuse is equal to the sum of the squares of the other two sides as it is that the hypotenuse is opposite the largest angle, nevertheless, once the former has been ascertained, it is no less believed. However, as far as God is concerned, if I were not overwhelmed by prejudices and if the images of sensible things were not besieging my thought from all directions, I would certainly acknowledge nothing sooner or more easily than him. For what, in and of itself, is more manifest than that a supreme being exists, that is, that God, to whose essence alone existence belongs, exists?

And although I needed to pay close attention in order to perceive this, nevertheless I now am just as certain about this as I am about everything else that seems most certain. Moreover, I observe also that certitude about other things is so dependent on this, that without it nothing can ever be perfectly known.

For I am indeed of such a nature that, while I perceive something very clearly and distinctly, I cannot help believing it to be true. Nevertheless, my nature is also such that I cannot focus my mental gaze always on the same thing, so as to perceive it clearly. Often the memory of a previously made judgment may return when I am no longer attending to the arguments on account of which I made such a judgment. Thus, other arguments can be brought forward that would easily make me change my opinion, were I ignorant of God. And thus I would never have true and certain knowledge about anything, but merely fickle and changeable opinions. Thus, for example, when I consider the nature of a triangle, it appears most evident to me, steeped as I am in the principles of geometry, that its three angles are equal to two right angles. And so long as I attend to its demonstration I cannot help believing this to be true. But no sooner do I turn the mind's eye away from the demonstration, than, however much I still recall that I had observed it most clearly, nevertheless, it can easily happen that I entertain doubts about whether it is true, were I ignorant of God. For I can convince myself that I have been so constituted by nature that I might occasionally be mistaken about those things I believe I perceive most evidently, especially when I recall that I have often taken many things to be true and certain, which other arguments have subsequently led me to judge to be false.

But once I perceived that there is a God, and also understood at the same time that everything else depends on him, and that he is not a deceiver, I then concluded that everything that I clearly and distinctly perceive is necessarily true. Hence even if I no longer attend to the reasons leading me to judge this to be true, so long as I merely recall that I did clearly and distinctly observe it, no counter-argument can be brought forward that might force me to doubt it. On the contrary, I have a true and certain knowledge of it. And not just of this one fact, but of everything else that I recall once having demonstrated, as in geometry, and so on.

For what objections can now be raised against me? That I have been made such that I am often mistaken? But I now know that I cannot be mistaken in matters I plainly understand. That I have taken many things to be true and certain which subsequently I recognized to be false? But none of these were things I clearly and distinctly perceived. But I was ignorant of this rule for determining the truth, and I believed these things perhaps for other reasons which I later discovered were less firm. What then remains to be said? That perhaps I am dreaming, as I recently objected against myself, in other words, that everything I am now thinking of is no truer than what occurs to someone who is asleep? Be that as it may, this changes nothing; for certainly, even if I were dreaming, if anything is evident to my intellect, then it is entirely true.

And thus I see plainly that the certainty and truth of every science depends exclusively upon the knowledge of the true God, to the extent that, prior to my becoming aware of him, I was incapable of achieving perfect knowledge about anything else. But now it is possible for me to achieve full and certain knowledge about countless things, both about God and other intellectual matters, as well as about the entirety of that corporeal nature which is the object of pure mathematics.

MEDITATION SIX: Concerning the Existence of Material Things, and the Real Distinction between Mind and Body

It remains for me to examine whether material things exist. Indeed I now know that they can exist, at least insofar as they are the object of pure mathematics, since I clearly and distinctly perceive them. For no doubt God is capable of bringing about everything that I am capable of perceiving in this way. And I have never judged that God was incapable of something, except when it was incompatible with my perceiving it distinctly. Moreover, from the faculty of imagination, which I notice I use while dealing with material things, it seems to follow that they exist. For to anyone paying very close attention to what imagination is, it appears to be simply a certain application of the knowing faculty to a body intimately present to it, and which therefore exists.

To make this clear, I first examine the difference between imagination and pure intellection. So, for example, when I imagine a triangle, I not only understand that it is a figure bounded by three lines, but at the same time I also envisage with the mind's eye those lines as if they were present; and this is what I call "imagining." On the other hand, if I want to think about a chiliagon, I certainly understand that it is a figure consisting of a thousand sides, just as well as I understand that a triangle is a figure consisting of three sides, yet I do not imagine those thousand sides in the same way, or envisage them as if they were present. And although in that case—because of force of habit I always imagine something whenever I think about a corporeal thing—I may perchance represent to myself some figure in a confused fashion, nevertheless this figure is obviously not a chiliagon. For this figure is really no different from the figure I would represent to myself, were I thinking of a myriagon or any other figure with a large number of sides. Nor is this figure of any help in knowing the properties that differentiate a chiliagon from other polygons. But if the figure in question is a pentagon, I surely can understand its figure, just as was the case with the chiliagon, without the help of my imagination. But I can also imagine a pentagon by turning the mind's eye both to its five sides and at the same time to the area bounded by those sides. At this point I am manifestly aware that I am in need of a peculiar sort of effort on the part of the mind in order to imagine, one that I do not employ in order to understand. This new effort on the part of the mind clearly shows the difference between imagination and pure intellection.

Moreover, I consider that this power of imagining that is in me, insofar as it differs from the power of understanding, is not required for my own essence, that is, the essence of my mind. For were I to be lacking this power, I would nevertheless undoubtedly remain the same entity I am now. Thus it seems to follow that the power of imagining depends upon something distinct from me. And I readily understand that, were a body to exist to which a mind is so joined that it may apply itself in order, as it were, to look at it any time it wishes, it could happen that it is by means of this very body that I imagine corporeal things. As a result, this mode of thinking may differ from pure intellection only in the sense that the mind, when it understands, in a sense turns toward itself and looks at one of the ideas that are in it; whereas when it imagines, it turns toward the body, and intuits in the body something that conforms to an idea either understood by the mind or perceived by sense. To be sure, I easily understand that the imagination can be actualized in this way, provided a body does exist. And since I can think of no other way of explaining imagination that is equally appropriate, I make a probable conjecture from this that a body exists. But this is only a probability. And even though I may examine everything carefully, nevertheless I do not yet see how the distinct idea of corporeal nature that I find in my imagination can enable me to develop an argument which necessarily concludes that some body exists.

But I am in the habit of imagining many other things, over and above that corporeal nature which is the object of pure mathematics, such as colors, sounds, tastes, pain, and the like, though not so distinctly. And I perceive these things better by means of the senses, from which, with the aid of the memory, they seem to have arrived at the imagination. Thus

I should pay the same degree of attention to the senses, so that I might deal with them more appropriately. I must see whether I can obtain any reliable argument for the existence of corporeal things from those things that are perceived by the mode of thinking that I call "sense."

First of all, to be sure, I will review here all the things I previously believed to be true because I had perceived them by means of the senses and the causes I had for thinking this. Next I will assess the causes why I later called them into doubt. Finally, I will consider what I must now believe about these things.

So first, I sensed that I had a head, hands, feet, and other members that comprised this body which I viewed as part of me, or perhaps even as the whole of me. I sensed that this body was found among many other bodies, by which my body can be affected in various beneficial or harmful ways. I gauged what was opportune by means of a certain sensation of pleasure, and what was inopportune by a sensation of pain. In addition to pain and pleasure, I also sensed within me hunger, thirst, and other such appetites, as well as certain bodily tendencies toward mirth, sadness, anger, and other such affects. And externally, besides the extension, shapes, and motions of bodies, I also sensed their hardness, heat, and other tactile qualities. I also sensed light, colors, odors, tastes, and sounds, on the basis of whose variety I distinguished the sky, the earth, the seas, and the other bodies, one from the other. Now given the ideas of all these qualities that presented themselves to my thought, and which were all that I properly and immediately sensed, still it was surely not without reason that I thought I sensed things that were manifestly different from my thought, namely, the bodies from which these ideas proceeded. For I knew by experience that these ideas came upon me utterly without my consent, to the extent that, wish as I may, I could not sense any object unless it was present to a sense organ. Nor could I fail to sense it when it was present. And since the ideas perceived by sense were much more vivid and explicit and even, in their own way, more distinct than any of those that I deliberately and knowingly formed through meditation or that I found impressed on my memory, it seemed impossible that they came from myself. Thus the remaining alternative was that they came from other things. Since I had no knowledge of such things except from those same ideas themselves, I could not help entertaining the thought that they were similar to those ideas. Moreover, I also recalled that the use of the senses antedated the use of reason. And since I saw that the ideas that I myself fashioned were not as explicit as those that I perceived through the faculty of sense, and were for the most part composed of parts of the latter, I easily convinced myself that I had absolutely no idea in the intellect that I did not have beforehand in the sense faculty. Not without reason did I judge that this body, which by a certain special right I called "mine," belongs more to me than did any other. For I could never be separated from it in the same way I could be from other bodies. I sensed all appetites and feelings in and on behalf of it. Finally, I noticed pain and pleasurable excitement in its parts, but not in other bodies external to it. But why should a certain sadness of spirit arise from some sensation or other of pain, and why should a certain elation arise from a sensation of excitement, or why should that peculiar twitching in the stomach, which I call hunger, warn me to have something to eat, or why should dryness in the throat warn me to take something to drink, and so on? I plainly had no explanation other than that I had been taught this way by nature. For there is no affinity whatsoever, at least none I am aware of, between this twitching in the stomach and the will to have something to eat, or between the sensation of something causing pain and the thought of sadness arising from this sensation. But nature also seems to have taught me everything else as well that I judged concerning the objects of the senses, for I had already convinced myself that this was how things were, prior to my assessing any of the arguments that might prove it.

Afterwards, however, many experiences gradually weakened any faith that I had in the senses. Towers that had seemed round from afar occasionally appeared square at close quarters. Very large statues mounted on their pedestals did not seem large to someone looking at them from ground level. And in countless other such instances I determined that judgments in matters of the external senses were in error. And not just the external senses, but the internal senses as well. For what can be more intimate than pain? But I had sometimes heard it said by people whose leg or arm had been amputated that it seemed to them that they still occasionally sensed pain in the very limb they had lost. Thus, even in my own case it did not seem to be entirely certain that some bodily member was causing me pain, even though I did sense pain in it. To these causes for doubt I recently added two quite general ones. The first was that everything I ever thought I sensed while awake I could believe I also sometimes sensed while asleep, and since I do not believe that what I seem to sense in my dreams comes to me from things external to me, I saw no reason why I should hold this belief about those things I seem to be sensing while awake. The second was that, since I was still ignorant of the author of my origin (or at least pretended to be ignorant of it), I saw nothing to prevent my having been so constituted by nature that I should be mistaken even about what seemed to me most true. As to the arguments that used to convince me of the truth of sensible things, I found no difficulty responding to them. For since I seemed driven by nature toward many things about which reason tried to dissuade me, I did not think that what

I was taught by nature deserved much credence. And even though the perceptions of the senses did not depend on my will, I did not think that we must therefore conclude that they came from things distinct from me, since perhaps there is some faculty in me, as yet unknown to me, that produces these perceptions.

But now, having begun to have a better knowledge of myself and the author of my origin, I am of the opinion that I must not rashly admit everything that I seem to derive from the senses; but neither, for that matter, should I call everything into doubt.

First, I know that all the things that I clearly and distinctly understand can be made by God such as I understand them. For this reason, my ability clearly and distinctly to understand one thing without another suffices to make me certain that the one thing is different from the other, since they can be separated from each other, at least by God. The question as to the sort of power that might effect such a separation is not relevant to their being thought to be different. For this reason, from the fact that I know that I exist, and that at the same time I judge that obviously nothing else belongs to my nature or essence except that I am a thinking thing, I rightly conclude that my essence consists entirely in my being a thinking thing. And although perhaps (or rather, as I shall soon say, assuredly) I have a body that is very closely joined to me, nevertheless, because on the one hand I have a clear and distinct idea of myself, insofar as I am merely a thinking thing and not an extended thing, and because on the other hand I have a distinct idea of a body, insofar as it is merely an extended thing and not a thinking thing, it is certain that I am really distinct from my body, and can exist without it.

Moreover, I find in myself faculties for certain special modes of thinking, namely the faculties of imagining and sensing. I can clearly and distinctly understand myself in my entirety without these faculties, but not vice versa: I cannot understand them clearly and distinctly without me, that is, without a substance endowed with understanding in which they inhere, for they include an act of understanding in their formal concept. Thus I perceive them to be distinguished from me as modes from a thing. I also acknowledge that there are certain other faculties, such as those of moving from one place to another, of taking on various shapes, and so on, that, like sensing or imagining, cannot be understood apart from some substance in which they inhere, and hence without which they cannot exist. But it is clear that these faculties, if in fact they exist, must be in a corporeal or extended substance, not in a substance endowed with understanding. For some extension is contained in a clear and distinct concept of them, though certainly not any understanding. Now there clearly is in me a passive faculty of sensing, that is, a faculty for receiving and knowing the ideas of sensible things; but I could not use it unless there also existed, either in me or in something else, a certain active faculty of producing or bringing about these ideas. But this faculty surely cannot be in me, since it clearly presupposes no act of understanding, and these ideas are produced without my cooperation and often even against my will. Therefore the only alternative is that it is in some substance different from me, containing either formally or eminently all the reality that exists objectively in the ideas produced by that faculty, as I have just noted above. Hence this substance is either a body, that is, a corporeal nature, which contains formally all that is contained objectively in the ideas, or else it is God, or some other creature more noble than a body, which contains eminently all that is contained objectively in the ideas. But since God is not a deceiver, it is patently obvious that he does not send me these ideas either immediately by himself, or even through the mediation of some creature that contains the objective reality of these ideas not formally but only eminently. For since God has given me no faculty whatsoever for making this determination, but instead has given me a great inclination to believe that these ideas issue from corporeal things, I fail to see how God could be understood not to be a deceiver, if these ideas were to issue from a source other than corporeal things. And consequently corporeal things exist. Nevertheless, perhaps not all bodies exist exactly as I grasp them by sense, since this sensory grasp is in many cases very obscure and confused. But at least they do contain everything I clearly and distinctly understand—that is, everything, considered in a general sense, that is encompassed in the object of pure mathematics.

As far as the remaining matters are concerned, which are either merely particular (for example, that the sun is of such and such a size or shape, and so on) or less clearly understood (for example, light, sound, pain, and the like), even though these matters are very doubtful and uncertain, nevertheless the fact that God is no deceiver (and thus no falsity can be found in my opinions, unless there is also in me a faculty given me by God for the purpose of rectifying this falsity) offers me a definite hope of reaching the truth even in these matters. And surely there is no doubt that all that I am taught by nature has some truth to it; for by "nature," taken generally, I understand nothing other than God himself or the ordered network of created things which was instituted by God. By my own particular nature I understand nothing other than the combination of all the things bestowed upon me by God.

There is nothing that this nature teaches me more explicitly than that I have a body that is ill-disposed when I feel pain, that needs food and drink when I suffer hunger or thirst, and the like. Therefore, I should not doubt that there is some truth in this.

81   By means of these sensations of pain, hunger, thirst and so on, nature also teaches that I am present not merely to my body in the way a sailor is present in a ship, but that I am most tightly joined and, so to speak, commingled with it, so much so that I and the body constitute one single thing. For if this were not the case, then I, who am only a thinking thing, would not sense pain when the body is injured; rather, I would perceive the wound by means of the pure intellect, just as a sailor perceives by sight whether anything in his ship is broken. And when the body is in need of food or drink, I should understand this explicitly, instead of having confused sensations of hunger and thirst. For clearly these sensations of thirst, hunger, pain, and so on are nothing but certain confused modes of thinking arising from the union and, as it were, the commingling of the mind with the body.

    Moreover, I am also taught by nature that various other bodies exist around my body, some of which are to be pursued, while others are to be avoided. And to be sure, from the fact that I sense a wide variety of colors, sounds, odors, tastes, levels of heat, and grades of roughness, and the like, I rightly conclude that in the bodies from which these different perceptions of the senses proceed there are differences corresponding to the different perceptions—though perhaps the latter do not resemble the former. And from the fact that some of these perceptions are pleasant while others are unpleasant, it is plainly certain that my body, or rather my whole self, insofar as I am comprised of a body and a mind, can be affected by various beneficial and harmful bodies in the vicinity.

82   Granted, there are many other things that I seem to have been taught by nature; nevertheless it was not really nature that taught them to me but a certain habit of making reckless judgments. And thus it could easily happen that these judgments are false: for example, that any space where there is absolutely nothing happening to move my senses is empty; or that there is something in a hot body that bears an exact likeness to the idea of heat that is in me; or that in a white or green body there is the same whiteness or greenness that I sense; or that in a bitter or sweet body there is the same taste, and so on; or that stars and towers and any other distant bodies have the same size and shape that they present to my senses, and other things of this sort. But to ensure that my perceptions in this matter are sufficiently distinct, I ought to define more precisely what exactly I mean when I say that I am "taught something by nature." For I am taking "nature" here more narrowly than the combination of everything bestowed on me by God. For this combination embraces many things that belong exclusively to my mind, such as my perceiving that what has been done cannot be undone, and everything else that is known by the light of nature. That is not what I am talking about here. There are also many things that belong exclusively to the body, such as that it tends to move downward, and so on. I am not dealing with these either, but only with what God has bestowed on me insofar as I am composed of mind and body. Accordingly, it is this nature that teaches me to avoid things that produce a sensation of pain and to pursue things that produce a sensation of pleasure, and the like. But it does not appear that nature teaches us to conclude anything, besides these things, from these sense perceptions unless the intellect has first conducted its own inquiry regarding things external to us. For it seems to belong exclusively to the mind, and not to the composite of mind and body, to know the truth in these matters. Thus, although a star affects my eye no more than does the flame from a small torch, still there is no real or positive tendency in my eye toward believing that the star is no larger than the flame. Yet, ever since my youth, I have made this judgment without any reason for doing so. And although I feel heat as I draw closer to the fire, and I also feel pain upon drawing too close to it, there is not a single argument that persuades me that there is something in the fire similar to that heat, any more than to that pain. On the contrary, I am convinced only that there is something in the fire that, regardless of what it finally turns out to be, causes in us those sensations of heat or pain. And although there may be nothing in a given space that moves the senses, it does not therefore follow that there is no body in it. But I see that in these and many other instances I have been in the habit of subverting the order of nature. For admittedly I use the perceptions of the senses (which are properly given by nature only for signifying to the mind what things are useful or harmful to the composite of which it is a part, and to that extent they are clear and distinct enough) as reliable rules for immediately discerning what is the essence of bodies located outside us. Yet they signify nothing about that except quite obscurely and confusedly.

I have already examined in sufficient detail how it could happen that my judgments are false, despite the goodness of God. But a new difficulty now arises regarding those very things that nature shows me are either to be sought out or avoided, as well as the internal sensations where I seem to have detected errors, as for example, when someone is deluded by a food's pleasant taste to eat the poison hidden inside it. In this case, however, he is driven by nature only toward desiring the thing in which the pleasurable taste is found, but not toward the poison, of which he obviously is unaware. I can only conclude that this nature is not omniscient. This is not remarkable, since man is a limited thing, and thus only what is of limited perfection befits him.

But we not infrequently err even in those things to which nature impels us. Take, for example, the case of those who are ill and who desire food or drink that will soon afterwards be injurious to them. Perhaps it could be said here that they erred because their nature was corrupt. However, this does not remove our difficulty, for a sick man is no less a creature of God than a healthy one, and thus it seems no less inconsistent that the sick man got a deception-prone nature from God. And a clock made of wheels and counter-weights follows all the laws of nature no less closely when it has been badly constructed and does not tell time accurately than it does when it completely satisfies the wish of its maker. Likewise, I might regard a man's body as a kind of mechanism that is outfitted with and composed of bones, nerves, muscles, veins, blood and skin in such a way that, even if no mind existed in it, the man's body would still exhibit all the same motions that are in it now except for those motions that proceed either from a command of the will or, consequently, from the mind. I easily recognize that it would be natural for this body, were it, say, suffering from dropsy and experiencing dryness in the throat (which typically produces a thirst sensation in the mind), and also so disposed by its nerves and other parts to take something to drink, the result of which would be to exacerbate the illness. This is as natural as for a body without any such illness to be moved by the same dryness in the throat to take something to drink that is useful to it. And given the intended purpose of the clock, I could say that it deviates from its nature when it fails to tell the right time. And similarly, considering the mechanism of the human body in terms of its being equipped for the motions that typically occur in it, I may think that it too is deviating from its nature, if its throat were dry when having something to drink is not beneficial to its conservation. Nevertheless, I am well aware that this last use of "nature" differs greatly from the other. For this latter "nature" is merely a designation dependent on my thought, since it compares a man in poor health and a poorly constructed clock with the ideas of a healthy man and of a well-made clock, a designation extrinsic to the things to which it is applied. But by "nature" taken in the former sense, I understand something that is really in things, and thus is not without some truth.

When we say, then, in the case of the body suffering from dropsy, that its "nature" is corrupt, given the fact that it has a parched throat and yet does not need something to drink, "nature" obviously is merely an extrinsic designation. Nevertheless, in the case of the composite, that is, of a mind joined to such a body, it is not a mere designation, but a true error of nature that this body should be thirsty when having something to drink would be harmful to it. It therefore remains to inquire here how the goodness of God does not prevent "nature," thus considered, from being deceptive.

Now my first observation here is that there is a great difference between a mind and a body in that a body, by its very nature, is always divisible. On the other hand, the mind is utterly indivisible. For when I consider the mind, that is, myself insofar as I am only a thinking thing, I cannot distinguish any parts within me; rather, I understand myself to be manifestly one complete thing. Although the entire mind seems to be united to the entire body, nevertheless, were a foot or an arm or any other bodily part to be amputated, I know that nothing has been taken away from the mind on that account. Nor can the faculties of willing, sensing, understanding, and so on be called "parts" of the mind, since it is one and the same mind that wills, senses, and understands. On the other hand, there is no corporeal or extended thing I can think of that I may not in my thought easily divide into parts; and in this way I understand that it is divisible. This consideration alone would suffice to teach me that the mind is wholly diverse from the body, had I not yet known it well enough in any other way.

My second observation is that my mind is not immediately affected by all the parts of the body, but only by the brain, or perhaps even by just one small part of the brain, namely, by that part where the "common" sense is said to reside. Whenever this part of the brain is disposed in the same manner, it presents the same thing to the mind, even if the other parts of the body are able meanwhile to be related in diverse ways. Countless experiments show this, none of which need be reviewed here.

My next observation is that the nature of the body is such that whenever any of its parts can be moved by another part some distance away, it can also be moved in the same manner by any of the parts that lie between them, even if this more distant part is doing nothing. For example, in the cord ABCD, if the final part D is pulled, the first part A would be moved in exactly the same manner as it could be, if one of the intermediate parts B or C were pulled, while the end part D remained immobile. Likewise, when I feel a pain in my foot, physics teaches me that this sensation took place by means of nerves distributed throughout the foot, like stretched cords extending from the foot all the way to the brain. When these nerves are pulled in the foot, they also pull on the inner parts of the brain to which they extend, and produce a certain motion in them. This motion has been constituted by nature so as to affect the mind with a sensation of pain, as if it occurred in the foot. But because these nerves need to pass through the shin, thigh, loins, back, and neck to get from the foot to the brain, it can happen that even if it is not the part in the foot but merely one of the intermediate parts that is being struck, the very same movement will occur in the brain that would occur were the foot badly injured. The inevitable result will be that the mind feels the same pain. The same opinion should hold for any other sensation.

My final observation is that, since any given motion occurring in that part of the brain immediately affecting the mind produces but one sensation in it, I can think of no better arrangement than that it produces the one sensation that, of all the ones it is able to produce, is most especially and most often conducive to the maintenance of a healthy man. Moreover, experience shows that all the sensations bestowed on us by nature are like this. Hence there is absolutely nothing to be found in them that does not bear witness to God's power and goodness. Thus, for example, when the nerves in the foot are agitated in a violent and unusual manner, this motion of theirs extends through the marrow of the spine to the inner reaches of the brain, where it gives the mind the sign to sense something, namely, the pain as if it is occurring in the foot. This provokes the mind to do its utmost to move away from the cause of the pain, since it is seen as harmful to the foot. But the nature of man could have been so constituted by God that this same motion in the brain might have indicated something else to the mind: for example, either the motion itself as it occurs in the brain, or in the foot, or in some place in between, or something else entirely different. But nothing else would have served so well the maintenance of the body. Similarly, when we need something to drink, a certain dryness arises in the throat that moves the nerves in the throat, and, by means of them, the inner parts of the brain. And this motion affects the mind with a sensation of thirst, because in this entire affair nothing is more useful for us to know than that we need something to drink in order to maintain our health; the same holds in the other cases.

From these considerations it is utterly apparent that, notwithstanding the immense goodness of God, the nature of man, insofar as it is composed of mind and body, cannot help being sometimes mistaken. For if some cause, not in the foot but in some other part through which the nerves extend from the foot to the brain, or perhaps even in the brain itself, were to produce the same motion that would normally be produced by a badly injured foot, the pain will be felt as if it were in the foot, and the senses will naturally be deceived. For since an identical motion in the brain can only bring about an identical sensation in the mind, and it is more frequently the case that this motion is wont to arise on account of a cause that harms the foot than on account of some other thing existing elsewhere, it is reasonable that the motion should always show pain to the mind as something belonging to the foot rather than to some other part. And if dryness in the throat does not arise, as is normal, because taking something to drink contributes to bodily health, but from a contrary cause, as happens in the case of someone with dropsy, then it is far better that it should deceive on that occasion than that it should always be deceptive when the body is in good health. The same holds for the other cases.

This consideration is most helpful, not only for my noticing all the errors to which my nature is liable, but also for enabling me to correct or avoid them without difficulty. To be sure, I know that all the senses set forth what is true more frequently than what is false regarding what concerns the welfare of the body. Moreover, I can nearly always make use of several of them in order to examine the same thing. Furthermore, I can use my memory, which connects current happenings with past ones, and my intellect, which now has examined all the causes of error. Hence I should no longer fear that those things that are daily shown me by the senses are false. On the contrary, the hyperbolic doubts of the last few days ought to be rejected as ludicrous. This goes especially for the chief reason for doubting, which dealt with my failure to distinguish being asleep from being awake. For I now notice that there is a considerable difference between these two; dreams are never joined by the memory with all the other actions of life, as is the case with those actions that occur when one is awake. For surely, if, while I am awake, someone were suddenly to appear to me and then immediately disappear, as occurs in dreams, so that I see neither where he came from nor where he went, it is not without reason that I would judge him to be a ghost or a phantom conjured up in my brain, rather than a true man. But when these things happen, and I notice distinctly where they come from, where they are now, and when they come to me, and when I connect my perception of them without interruption with the whole rest of my life, I am clearly certain that these perceptions have happened to me not while I was dreaming but while I was awake. Nor ought I have even the least doubt regarding the truth of these things, if, having mustered all the senses, in addition to my memory and my intellect, in order to examine them, nothing is passed on to me by one of these sources that conflicts with the others. For from the fact that God is no deceiver, it follows that I am in no way mistaken in these matters. But because the need to get things done does not always permit us the leisure for such a careful inquiry, we must confess that the life of man is apt to commit errors regarding particular things, and we must acknowledge the infirmity of our nature.